What People are Saying

"I met Tarsha when she was starting her career in e-commerce and branding in the hotel industry. I've seen Tarsha reach the palace of her dreams through hard work, strength of character and commitment to become the Marketing Lady she aspired to be. What a gift for all of us to learn from her directly through her disciplined approach to personal branding. Tarsha's book is an easy, fun read and her authentic, caring voice comes through in her effective advice."

Cary Broussard, Author, From Cinderella to CEO
and Founder of the Cinderella to CEO Awards

"*Making an Impact: How to Build a Powerful Personal Brand* is a great guide for individuals with the ambition to stand out in their discipline but who also need a framework to guide them to success. Tarsha Polk is a professional in this vein; she's positively impacted people, organizations, and businesses in their branding initiatives and I will highly recommend this book to all."

Matt Houston, Interim President, Dallas Black Chamber of Commerce and
Former Chairman of the Board

"*Making an Impact: How to Build a Powerful Personal Brand* is an easy to read, easily implemented outline of steps for aspiring entrepreneurs looking to define, create and launch their brand in an effective and powerful manner."

Dr. Carla Russo, PhD of Zen Wellness Academy

Making an Impact: How to Build a Powerful Personal Brand

Making an Impact: How to Build a Powerful Personal Brand

Tarsha Polk

Life On Purpose Publishing
SAN ANTONIO, TEXAS

Email: info@themarketinglady.com
Online: www.themarketinglady.com

All brand names and product names used in this book are trademarks, registered trademarks, or trade names of their respective holders.

This publication is designed to provide accurate and authoritative information in regard to the subject matter covered. It is sold with the understanding that neither the publisher nor the author is engaged in rendering legal or other professional services. If legal advice or other expert assistance is required, the services of a competent professional person should be sought.

—From a declaration of principles jointly adopted by a committee of the American Bar Association and a committee of publishers.

A Gap Closer ™ Publication
      A Division of Life on Purpose Publishing
      San Antonio, Texas

Ordering Information:
Quantity sales. Special discounts are available on quantity purchases by corporations, associations, and others. For details, contact the "Special Sales Department" at the email address above.

Making an Impact: How to Build a Powerful Personal Brand/ Tarsha Polk. —1st ed.
ISBN: 978-1-7336950-1-5

Dedication

This book is dedicated to my nephew, Daemon V. Person:
Your short time on earth made a lasting impact on many lives.
Rest in heaven, Sweetie.

Acknowledgments

WRITING A BOOK requires a village of people who truly want to see you succeed and who believe in you. This book is a journey of how I built my brand and the insight I've gained along the way.

I want to give a heartfelt thank you to the following people for their support and encouragement: my SiSTARS Mastermind group: Toni Harris Taylor, Gena Davis, Lisa Ann Landry, Star Bobatoon and Dr. Angela Massey.

Tracee and Chalonda for the years of love and support you've shown me throughout my entrepreneurial journey.

And a big thank you to Gregory L. Hearns for being my number one cheerleader, supporter and listening ear.

Contents

PART THREE: REDEFINE YOUR BRAND

Foreword

I HAD THE opportunity to meet Tarsha Polk in 2006 when she interviewed me at the *Black Enterprise Entrepreneurs Conference* in Dallas, TX. During that interview, we discussed how being the first and only African-American to win on the hit reality television show, *The Apprentice,* helped build my brand. Since then, we've crossed paths at various conferences, and I was even a guest on her Internet radio show. Over the years, I've observed how Tarsha has built her personal brand through her articles, Internet radio show, public speaking and constant visibility. She is a talented and driven professional with a very impressive personal *and* professional brand.

I was, therefore, delighted when Tarsha asked me to write a foreword for this book. I believe she has knowledge and insight on the topic and the tips she shares will be helpful to any entrepreneur trying to build a brand name for themselves. Prior to winning season four of *The Apprentice,* I co-founded BCT Partners, a multi-million-dollar research, training, consulting, technology and analytics firm. By the time I was 30, I had already launched five companies and I've written several books about entrepreneurship and innovation, so I know a lot about success and the strategies entrepreneurs use to achieve it. Some of the strategies she outlines in this book are the same strategies I've used to build my brand, including delivering a clear and consistent message, networking strategically, and positioning your brand as the top choice in your industry. That's why I think the tips and strategies Tarsha outlines in this book will take you from no brand visibility to a powerful brand that positively impacts the success of your company.

Most business owners don't see themselves as a personal brand, they focus on building their company's brand. I know firsthand how building a personal brand can impact the success of one's company. It has helped me to further establish myself as an international public speaker, award-winning author and media personality and, in doing so, grow BCT Partners into a successful social enterprise that has landed multimillion-dollar and multibillion-dollar contracts. If you are an owner of a company and wondering if you should step from behind the corporate brand and develop a personal brand, then this book is for you.

While most small businesses fail within the first three years, The Marketing Lady, LLC has weathered the storm for sixteen years providing training, coaching and consulting to business owners, career professionals and corporations. It is through her years of experience consulting with small business owners on marketing and business strategies that Tarsha shares her own journey building her brand and how she's helped other entrepreneurs do the same.

Making an Impact: How to Build a Powerful Personal Brand is filled with more than just marketing and branding concepts, it contains case studies, examples, and a downloadable action plan to help you apply the concepts to your business.

For the beginner, this book can be an invaluable tool, guiding you through selecting the right brand name, colors, and messages. If you have a brand, this book will teach you how to tell your brand story and elevate your networking game. For the more established brand, she'll take you through an exercise to evaluate the brand building skills you need to maintain your brand's position in the marketplace. And lastly, for the experienced entrepreneur, this book can serve as a useful reminder and checklist of important concepts and practices you once learned but may be forgotten.

Tarsha's useful advice and practical suggestions are right on target, such as looking beyond your outward brand to evaluate your internal brand (yourself) to ensure it is projecting confidence or making full use of your personal power by way of good influencing skills. This is real, learned-from-experience advice that Tarsha lays out in this book. It will be helpful to you regardless of the number of years you have been in business.

As you read a chapter, you may want to implement the recommendations she provides before moving on to the next chapter. This book is intended to help you develop your personal brand marketing plan. You'll also get a sense of Tarsha Polk, the person—and you may find yourself relating to some of the experiences she shares about her personal setbacks and accomplishments.

Tarsha has put in the hard work it takes to define, build and grow a personal brand. She's certified in personal brand assessments and studied personal branding from William Arruda, one of the nation's leading experts in personal branding. She provides you with advice that people would pay thousands of dollars to obtain. I hope that reading this book will be like hiring Tarsha as your personal branding coach.

During the interview Tarsha and I had back in 2006, she asked me "Are you dreaming bigger now that you have won *The Apprentice?*" I replied, "Yes." And that is one of the lessons I've learned in life: That it is better to begin with the premise that you can do anything than to end with the realization that you could have done something. I believe that if you follow the guidelines and techniques in this book you will make an impact in your business and your life, inspire others and dream bigger than ever before.

Dr. Randal Pinkett
Chairman and CEO of BCT Partners
Season 4 Winner of *The Apprentice*

Introduction

*"We are CEOs of our own companies: Me, Inc.
To be in business today, our most important job
is to be head marketer for the brand called you."*

Tom Peters

I F YOU ARE struggling with creating a personal brand that stands out and gets noticed, you have come to the right place. *Making an Impact: How to Build a Powerful Personal Brand* will show you step-by-step all the tactics you need to make your brand have an impact in the marketplace, so you naturally attract the opportunities to grow your business. This book contains examples of the techniques corporations use to build brands, case studies of clients who implemented techniques taught in this book, and low-cost ways to make your brand stand out. You'll no longer be confused about how to brand yourself after reading this book.

It's easy to think that personal branding is for celebrities or influential people. After all, we follow them on social media, read their articles or see them on T.V. and think there's this magic formula to creating a personal brand. The reality is everyone has a set of unique attributes that make them who they are. Those attributes can be positioned and packaged into a brand that has meaning, offers value, and contributes to the success of the company.

When you read this book, you'll realize you've been confusing your audience trying to be like your competition instead of creating a brand that aligns with your mission, vision, values and goals. You'll also realize that the secret formula lies within *you*—the authentic you! *Making an Impact: How to Build a Powerful Personal Brand* will help you define who you are, create an action plan and show you how to market yourself.

For the last 16 years, I have built and grown a brand called The Marketing Lady and I share with you how I did it. I share with you all the strategies and techniques I used with thousands of people whom I have coached and trained, who have read my book and articles, or who've hired me as their consultant. The secrets to a powerful personal brand are all in this book. You'll benefit from reading this book because you'll have a plan that makes the process of learning how to market yourself less terrifying.

If you are brand new to personal branding, read the first five chapters because it defines who you are and what your brand is meant to be. I encourage you to download the personal brand action plan using the links provided after each chapter. If you are familiar with personal branding but need strategies to create more visibility, I suggest you start with chapters 6 – 9. And if you are looking to improve your personal brand, read chapters 10 – 12. Throughout the book you will have actions steps you can take and a notes page to jot down how you can implement what you've just learned. You'll read testimonials from people who have followed the techniques in the book and gained improved results.

While building a recognizable brand takes time, commitment and consistency, you can successfully create one on your own or fast track your success, by working with a personal brand coach certified in giving brand assessments. Wherever possible, web site addresses of resources have been included. When you visit these sites, you'll find additional information to help you increase your success at personal branding. If you have questions that the book didn't answer or you need extra advice and inspiration, I've provided personal brand resources at the end of the book.

The personal brand tips and techniques you're about to read have proven results. Each chapter provides new secrets that will help you stand out so you can attract more opportunities. If you follow the strategies in this book, it's highly possible YOU will be in the top-of-mind position when someone needs your product or service.

Tarsha Polk
www.themarketinglady.com
Plano, Texas

PART 1

DEFINE YOUR BRAND

"If you are alive, there's a purpose for your life."

RICK WARREN

CHAPTER ONE

Brand Destiny

*"Potential is a priceless treasure, like gold. All of us have
gold hidden within, but we have to dig to get it out."*
Joyce Meyer

I CALL MYSELF an accidental entrepreneur. My goal was to
climb the corporate ladder of success and become a marketing
VP. I did everything right. I went to college, attended graduate
school, and was a top performer on my team at work. Then one
day, I realized the truth about corporate America when someone in the company determined whether I could advance my
career. While working on a special project team in the e-Business
division of a Fortune 500 company, I was also attending graduate
school to obtain my MBA with double concentrations in
Marketing and e-Business. The company was reimbursing my
tuition because I majored in something that I could apply within
their company. My efforts didn't go unnoticed.

Soon a position became available for which I was encour-
aged to apply. The position was a perfect opportunity for me to
utilize my soon-to-receive MBA education and apply what I'd
learned to the role. During the application process, my boss denied

me an internal transfer without good reason. To my boss, transferring me meant losing out on revenue and commission for the team. It meant having to assign my accounts to another person until a replacement was found. It also meant having to explain to upper management why I would be transferred in the middle of the quarter when I hadn't reached my sales goals yet.

It was at that moment I realized that someone else was in control of my destiny. I have to tell you I didn't like that at all! I realized that the organization didn't value me as an employee even though I had worked there for three years and had a great track record in the department. I was even nominated as Rookie of the Year my first year.

After taking the matter up the chain of command and contemplating my next move, two weeks later, I *fired my boss*. Soon after, I started my own marketing consultancy firm which led to creating the brand called The Marketing Lady.

My decision to quit was a leap of faith, but I was willing to take a risk and leave a situation where my gifts, talents, and skills were not being appreciated nor valued. I realized a great lesson from this pivotal moment in my journey that I want to share with you: The reason why personal and product brands fail to succeed is because they don't know their worth. They lack the confidence of knowing that what they have to offer is of value to someone in the marketplace.

Building Brand Confidence

I define brand confidence as the perception your audience has about your brand's abilities to deliver on its promises and trustworthiness. You can gain more of what you want and send stronger brand messages when you do so with confidence. A product or personal brand that appears wishy-washy has no influence over its intended audience. Be confident about your brand and the messages you send. Your brand consists of the key marketing message you want your target audience to hear, the quality of your work, and the images (logo, symbol, personal image) you want portrayed to connect customers to your brand. The most confident brands have several characteristics in common:

- They know who they are and understand how their brand impacts others. If you don't know your brand's purpose, you confuse your customers and your messages become unclear. I talk more about brand purpose in a later chapter.
- They listen to their audience and meet their needs or requirements. Sometimes brands are so focused on what they sell they miss the mark when it comes to identifying if they are meeting the needs and expectations of their customers.
- They project a professional and trustworthy image. 55% of communication is visual and if your brand doesn't look the part, customers won't trust doing business with you.
- They have a consistent core message. Are you clearly communicating the customer's problems or value proposition in your messages? Don Miller, author of Building a Story Brand says, "if you confuse you lose." So, if your messaging is not consistent and clear, customers won't buy from you.
- They convey their brand's value proposition. Corporate brands are more aware of the concept of value proposi-

tion than a personal brand. A value proposition is quite simple: why should a customer buy your product or use your service? It explains how your brand solves a problem or adds more value.

When you believe you have great ideas, a great product or service, or skills and talents to share with the world, you will have the confidence to position yourself or your product as a powerful brand. I'm going to show you how in the next few chapters, but first let's talk about fear.

Get Over Your Fear and Doubt

Running a business or building a brand can be scary because you have no idea whether the outcome will be a success or a failure. Any time you do something new or different that takes you out of your comfort zone, negative self-talk sets in. You start to doubt yourself, team, or even the product you offer. It's been said that fear is simply *false evidence appearing real*. Fear is an emotion we all deal with—we can handle it with anxiety or feel empowered to do something new. To overcome fear, you must have faith and outrageous confidence. You must have faith in God and yes . . . confidence in yourself. It is my belief that when you have faith and outrageous confidence, the stage will be set far beyond what you can imagine. If your desire is to achieve your goals and attain the next level of success as a powerful and influential brand, you must get over your fear.

Overcoming your fears so you can build a powerful brand requires you to train yourself to be more courageous. According to *Psychology Today*, there is evidence that says you can do so.

Here are some simple steps:

- Lean on your friends, family or a business support group. You can bounce ideas off them, ask them to be your test market, or get emotional support.
- Expose yourself to more of what you are afraid of. If positioning your brand means you must do public speaking, but you dread it, start by attending a *Toastmasters* meeting to hone your skills. *Toastmasters* is an organization that helps people become better speakers.
- Use positive self-talk when you have negative thoughts. We all have negative internal dialogue. We say something like, "I don't know the first thing about making people remember my brand." The more you think those negative thoughts, the more you start to believe them, and doubt sets in.
- Start small instead of trying to be a big brand right away. It can be discouraging when you have a big vision for your brand and so much to do to reach your goals. Take things one step at a time, so you don't feel overwhelmed or discouraged. When you've accomplished one small task towards building your brand, it will boost your confidence.

I coached a young woman who wanted to start a virtual assistance business but felt she didn't have enough skills to run it and get clients. The first thing I had her do was jot down a list of skills she had and how she used them in the past. We went through her list of skills and identified how they could be used in running a small business. I provided resources she could use to develop the skills she lacked, and we discussed outsourcing other skills.

She spent two months launching her business and working through her business plan. During the first 30 days she obtained a client and assisted them with a women's conference. Within the first six months, she had a furniture store and small business owner on retainer. I believe her early startup success came from knowing her strengths and how to leverage them. She overcame her fear and recognized her value.

Simply put, have faith in your strengths. Focus on what you or your brand is good at and spotlight the skills, education, experience, quality, and uniqueness of what you offer.

You must have confidence in your talents and position yourself as the "go-to" person or company for your expertise. Soon, you become the center of influence and the authority in your field.

Do a reality check and ask yourself, your customers, and your staff these questions:

- Who am I?
- What kind of company do I have?
- Where do I need to be?
- Where does my company need to be?

By answering these questions, you uncover your unique and distinct value proposition to separate your brand from the rest. This makes you stand out and people are attracted to confident brands.

Meet Tyger

One of my female clients is an account executive in the private charter jet industry. It's a male-dominated field one in which it's difficult for females to succeed. Even though she was a confident person by nature (they nicknamed her Tyger), she struggled to position herself in the field and stand out from her male coun-terparts. She had 18 years of experience working in the aviation and travel industry. She was driven, ambitious and had the same level of skill as her male counterparts. However, let's face it, be-ing a female in that industry can be intimidating. She came to me because she wanted to be known as the "go to person" amongst her colleagues and target audience.

My team and I did a reality check and asked her a few of the same questions I suggested to you earlier.

- Who are you? *She was an expert with 18 years of aviation experience. She was smart, ambitious and a skilled salesper-son.*
- What does your brand need to be? *It needed to be sophis-ticated and confident. Her clients were CEOs and wealthy people, so she had to be positioned in a way that they could count on her to provide them with a luxury jet to meet their unique needs.*

We branded her website, social media and marketing con-tent as an expert in private jet travel with the confidence her clients needed to help them with their luxury travel needs.

"Sending a big thank you, Tarsha, to you and your team for making me and my new brand look good. You're the best!"

Tywana 'Tyger' Greene
Expert in Private Jet Travel

Like Tyger, once you realize who you are and the expertise your company provides, you can and will become a powerful brand.

Chapter Summary

In the sixteen years I've been helping entrepreneurs, I've learned that most lack brand confidence which holds them back. It holds them back from taking their ideas to market, holds them back from promoting what they offer and, in some cases, causes them to quit.

Think beyond your outward brand and evaluate your internal brand (yourself) to ensure you, as the owner, creator or brand itself, are projecting confidence. Eliminate your fears and doubts by changing your mindset and focusing on your strengths. When you are confident in your personal brand and clear on the value you add, there are unlimited possibilities.

Go to http://bit.ly/PBactionplan2 and download a personal brand action plan to help you dive deeper into building your powerful brand.

(How can you use the lessons in this chapter to increase your confidence? Use this page to write down your ideas and insights.)

CHAPTER TWO

How Brands are Born

"If you are alive, there's a purpose for your life."
Rick Warren

QUIT MY corporate job in March of 2003 while in my last year of graduate school. I had no idea what I was going to do, but I knew that with my degree and six years of sales and marketing experience I was bound to find another job. So, I did what most people looking for work would do, I started networking. I had no idea then that this would be the start of my entrepreneurial journey. I networked from the sunup to the sundown; I attended chamber meetings and industry professional groups. Having a background in corporate sales and marketing meant I was used to meeting new people, prospecting, asking qualifying questions and exchanging information and resources. While networking to find a job, I constantly met small business owners struggling with how to get their brand online. (Remember, this was in the early 2000s when doing business online was still very new.)

Before I even started my business or had a business name, my brand was being birthed. While I was in job transition, I was frequently asked by small business owners to help with their marketing. One day, while at a networking event, a gentleman I'd met at a previous event approached me. He remembered I did marketing and said, "Hey, I've seen you around before! You're that marketing lady, aren't you?" He went on to say, "I need some marketing help. What are your fees?" That's when the light bulb went off. Remember, I wasn't networking to prospect for clients. I was networking to find a job, but instead I was inspired to start my own business. I decided to start a marketing consulting firm to assist small businesses with establishing an online presence to attract more clients.

Brand with Purpose

Initially, the purpose for my brand was to fulfill small business owners' need to understand how the Internet would help their business reach new heights. My sole reason to start the business was to make the money I needed to replace my corporate income. But, as time went on and my business evolved, I had to brand with purpose because I realized the services I provided impacted people to live their dreams through entrepreneurship.

What does your brand stand for? If you haven't developed a higher purpose, goal, or mission for your brand that goes beyond just "increasing profit" you are missing out on an important marketing opportunity.

Big Brands are Increasingly Purpose-Driven

In today's marketplace, socially responsible brands that include humanitarian goals in their mission statements have a clear competitive advantage, especially with the Millennial market.

The world's biggest brands have taken notice and are capitalizing on this market strategy. Consider these brands:

- Walmart aims to "save people money so they can live better."

- The Always #LikeAGirl video (aimed at helping raise the self-esteem of those making the transition into womanhood) went viral to the tune of 80 million views.

- Unilever (Dove) aims to increase the health and economic status of developing nations by getting 1 billion people to change their hand-washing habits to reduce infant deaths throughout the world.

Clearly, big brands are making an impact on humanity while simultaneously making an impact on their bottom line. There's no reason why you cannot do the same.

3 Reasons Why You Should Develop a Brand with a Purpose

1. Employees want to work for companies with a higher purpose: Employees enjoy working towards a common goal. This is important to millennials who will make up 51% of the workforce in a few years.

2. Customers want to support brands that reflect their personal values: Consider the rise of "lifestyle brands." Customers now see spending as a form of self-expression.

3. It can increase your bottom line: There are many ways in which adopting a socially responsible cause can increase profits. For example, companies that focus on energy conservation can see tangible reduction in energy costs. Brands that focus on developing countries can be

the first to enter new markets. Socially conscious marketing campaigns with emotional appeals are more likely to go viral.

Develop Your Brand's Purpose

William Barclay said, "There are two great days in a person's life—the day we are born and the day we discover why." To develop your brand's purpose, pick a cause (your why) that aligns with your business and matters to your target audience. It should have an authentic relation to your business objectives. You can leverage your brand's purpose to attract and retain top talent, build long-term relationships with customers, and create viral marketing opportunities.

It might not be easy to figure out what your brand purpose is. Ask yourself what is the thing, work, mission that drives you to do what you do? What is the problem you want your business to solve? How can your company make a difference? And, who would benefit from what you do? Think long and hard about these questions. Meet with your team or a business coach to brainstorm the answers.

I've been talking mostly about product or service brands and how they are born, but the same applies to personal brands as well. The major difference is that a personal brand focuses more on the person and not the product or service the person offers. According to the Small Business Administration of Advocacy Report of 2012, 78.5 percent of U.S. businesses are non-employer firms. This means over three quarters of U.S. based small firms are run by solopreneurs. Wow, that's a lot of personal brands!

Exactly What is Personal Branding?

In 2005, when I changed my company name from Pivotal Marketing Group to The Marketing Lady, I didn't know that was the start of creating a personal brand. I wasn't familiar with the terminology then. I just knew that my prospective customers were attracted to my public persona more than the company brand. Other people were forming their own perceptions about my personal brand. They formed their own beliefs of what my brand stood for and why I created my business. What I learned through my training and certification with 360Reach™ Personal Branding is that personal branding involves communicating your values, beliefs, goals, and purpose in a way that makes you stand out.

360Reach™ is a web-based personal branding assessment that has been used by nearly a million people to understand how you are perceived by those around you. It gives you the critical feedback you need so you can expand your career or business success.

I used the 360Reach™ Personal Brand assessment tool to help me take more control of what my brand meant and how I wanted it to be perceived in the marketplace. What I found out was that the way I thought I showed up in the marketplace was different from how I was being perceived. Based on the feedback from my peers, friends and clients their opinion of my personal brand was associated with the luxury of a Lexus. According to the *2018 U.S. News and World Report*, 10 Best Luxury Car Brands, Lexus brands rank #6. I was marketing my brand like a Honda to an audience of Honda buyers. Although a Honda is a great car, it carries a different meaning and perception than Lexus. Through that assessment, I learned that I had to change the way I saw myself. I had to change my target audience and position the Marketing Lady brand as a luxury brand with an audience who were luxury buyers.

Now, I can better control the narrative of my brand and show my target audience what I want them to perceive about *The Marketing Lady*. Personal branding is about being authentic and showing up in an authentic way. So, in 2012, I shifted my primary focus to coaching solo-entrepreneurs and career professionals on how to define, create and launch their own personal brand.

A personal branding assessment allows me to view feedback from a client's peers and feedback on how they see their own personal brand. I'm able to look at their brand personality, attributes, core values and purpose to help them birth a unique personal brand.

One of the reasons I changed my company name from Pivotal Marketing Group to The Marketing Lady was because back then what I offered was not different from the competition. What my customers were buying into was *me*. My personal brand was the differentiating factor in their buying decision. Once I changed the name, more solopreneurs became interested in learning how they too could brand themselves. Entrepreneurs started to take notice of how I branded myself, how I was marketing myself and how my personal brand was becoming more influential.

In today's marketplace becoming a personal brand is about becoming an influencer marketer. Because of how the Kardashians and other celebrities have built personal brands online, individuals and entrepreneurs are becoming instafamous through social media and getting paid well to do so.

Meet Charmeachelle "Mike" Moore

"Before working with Ms. Polk, I really didn't have a vision of what I wanted my brand to look like or how the marketing world worked. I always knew the key principles of what I wanted my brand to stand for, but I never really knew anything about them. Ms. Polk opened my eyes to how branding and marketing worked. She introduced me to people that helped give me the idea and the branding position that I'm in now.

I didn't really expect things to move as quickly as they did when working with Ms. Polk. Immediately after our first meeting, she went to work contacting the people she felt would want to do business to me. She also exposed me to fellow athletes that were once in the same position but were older than me when they started their journey on marketing and branding. They were blown away that I was starting at an early age. Ms. Polk linked me with ex-players that played in the NFL and also in the NBA. She also connected me with the two amazing brothers who started the Rise company. I was able to work with and learn a lot from them about branding and sticking to what I stand for.

While working with Ms. Polk, she exposed me to and motivated me to work in my community and go global with my marketing. She helped me to think outside the box. She was able to show me that I could make money with branding and marketing and give back to my community and help people reach their full potential through sharing the things I experienced in my life. By setting up a small speaking engagement I was able to share my story and really challenge the youth to never give up and to go after whatever they want in life.

Ms. Polk helped build my confidence to see that I'm much more than a football player. She told me and showed me how I could change people's views about athletes. When referring people to Ms. Polk, I tell them to go in with an open mind and be ready to be challenged to think outside the box and watch how she works to

> *pull everything out of you to see yourself for more than who you are. She's able to give birth to your vision and help structure it in the right way for you to become successful."*
>
> Charmeachelle "Mike" Moore
> Former Linebacker, Los Angeles Chargers

Mike was later able to leverage his brand story and position himself to work with the *Player's Tribune Magazine* during the off season. Because of his amazing story and how he positioned his brand, he's exposing his brand in the media field which increases brand recognition.

You Were Born to Impact and Inspire

Mike Moore's story is one of overcoming tragedies and setbacks at a young age. His faith, determination, and positive attitude are what helped him overcome and go from a brain tumor diagnosis *and* the loss of his father to getting signed by the LA Chargers and then suffering from an injury while playing. Through all his trials and tribulations, he continued to post positive and inspirational messages on social media. He shared his story with children and other athletes. So, what does his personal brand stand for? It stands for determination and not quitting on your dreams regardless of the circumstances.

Chapter Summary

Brands can be born with intention or by accident, like mine. Just like every human was placed on this earth to serve a purpose (whether you know yours or not), your brand must have a purpose, so it can have an impact on your customers and key stakeholders.

Whether you have a company brand or a personal brand, define its purpose and live that purpose every day. Brands are born from our personality and attributes, our core meaning and what we are known for.

Go to http://bit.ly/PBactionplan2 and download a personal brand action plan to help you dive deeper into building your powerful brand.

(How can you use the lessons in this chapter to birth your brand? Use this page to write down your ideas and insights.)

CHAPTER THREE

Personal Brands are Influencers

*"Everyone is influencing the people around them
one way or another."*
Robin S. Sharma

OST PEOPLE THINK of celebrities when you say, influential personal brand. Why? Because they are well-known in their field, they have power, money, and respect. They have written books, done public speaking and even have television or radio shows. And, with all of that, they can influence people, situations, and attract customers just by marketing themselves and what they are known for. These celebrities have developed their own personal brands and packaged their unique attributes to market themselves.

They have been able to brand their skills and knowledge like Daymond John, who started an urban clothing line called FUBU in the early 90's. He built his personal brand around his skills of launching successful companies. Now, he is one of the "sharks" on the television show *Shark Tank*. He travels across the country doing workshops teaching people how to launch successful companies. Richard Branson, founder of Virgin Group, has a reputation for being a risk taker and having a fun personality. He has leveraged both elements to help expand the Virgin brand into several companies. Another great example of a personal brand is the Kardashians. Unlike the celebrities mentioned above, these women didn't build a brand around their experience, background or a specific talent, they became influential brands because of their personalities, lifestyle and popularity on social media. The Kardashian clan is skilled at influencing customers to buy their brands, follow them on social media, and buy brands that they endorse. In fact, four of the Kardashian sisters are listed as the highest paid social media influencers.

Influence is the ability to get voluntary cooperation from people while avoiding the tendency to manipulate. Manipulation is getting someone to do something or give you something that you want without regard to how they feel about it. Being influential simply means having an impact in the lives of people that engage with you.

You may or may not have the positional power or direct authority to gain the cooperation you need; however, it is possible to have personal power with good influencing skills.

Develop the Qualities and Skills to Build an Influential Brand

Do you know how the top 13% build their business, their influence and standout in the marketplace? They have become experts at developing the core qualities which are essential to building a personal brand that influences to attract clients and opportunities.

Influencer Qualities

Think about some of the brands you buy and their qualities or characteristics that compel you to buy. All brands have a meaning. All brands have a personality. All brands have an attitude. As consumers we often identify with, relate to, and define ourselves by their meaning, personality, and attitude; therefore, brands have influence. Here's what that influence comes down to:

- Emotional connection to customers - For a brand to succeed it must evoke an emotional attachment from its customers. For example, my allergist has a very laid back and caring personality. Each time I visit her office, I'm made to feel like I'm a friend, not just her patient. Because of this, I'm willing to wait 30 – 45 minutes before I can see her.

- An appealing personality - Every brand has a personality. When you think of Southwest Airlines you might think of fun and laid back, but when you think of American Airlines, you might think professional and corporate. A personal brand would promote a key attribute about themselves or personality to build their brand.

- Consistent value delivery – People are attracted to the value you promise to deliver. Based on your personality, special skills, and your purpose, what value can you promise to deliver to your target audience that your competitors cannot? Personal branding is about what makes you different and unique from others. Once you discover the things that make you different, you'll see they are the same things that make you valuable. What makes my allergist valuable to me is that she has great bedside manner every time I see her—better than any doctor I've ever had. When you read her reviews, you find patients saying similar things about their experiences.

- Trustworthiness – When brands consistently demonstrate behaviors that are aligned with the value they deliver, it builds trust. The more consistent you are, the more people trust that you are authentic. They trust that you'll do what you promised.

What's Your Influencer Style

Learning how you, as a personal brand, impact the opinions, ideas and actions of others will assist you in becoming more effective at influencing others. According to Discovering Learning International, the creators of the Influencer Style Assessment Tool, there are five influencing styles: Asserting, Inspiring, Bridging, Negotiating, and Rationalizing. The assessment tool classifies your influencer style based on answers to questions about preferred influencing tactics.

1. Asserting: Do you make sure your ideas are heard and considered? This style is valuable because you clearly communicate your stand on an issue.
2. Inspiring: Do you encourage others to share their ideas and help people see the possibilities? This style is valuable because of your ability to appeal to common hopes and aspirations.
3. Bridging: Do you influence others by building relationships, connecting and uniting with others to make sure they are heard and understood? This style is valuable because you build trust through open communication and acceptance of interest.

4. Negotiating: Do you encourage discussion around ideas and then negotiate an outcome that will satisfy your interest? This style is valuable because it helps people come to an agreement.
5. Rationalizing: Do you use facts to come to a logical solution? This style is valuable because you use accurate facts to base your position.

In the 1950s there was this popular jazz club in Hollywood called Mocambo. Many of the Hollywood elite would spend their nights there, including celebrities Frank Sinatra, Humphrey Bogart, and Clark Gable. The critically acclaimed jazz singer, Ella Fitzgerald, had difficulty convincing the club manager to book her there because the venue appealed to mostly white audiences. What the club owner didn't know was that Ella was good friends with Hollywood influencer, Marilyn Monroe. Ella told Marilyn her frustration about singing at Mocambo. Marilyn called the manager of the club and asked him to book Ella. She told him that if he made Ella the headliner of Mocambo for a week, she'd sit in the front row every night Ella was there. Thinking about the amount of press and attention the club would get if Marilyn Monroe was there, he agreed to make Ella the headliner. Not only did that phone call elevate the career of Ella Fitzgerald; it also broke racial barriers.

This story is a great example of personal branding using the "negotiating" influencer style. You and I may not have the influencing power of Marilyn Monroe or the vocals of Ella Fitzgerald, but we can still learn a lot from what they were able to do at Mocambo. When we want to influence people or the world, we must pay attention to where our power lies and anticipate objections to our proposals with ready-made solutions that are hard to turn down.

The success of your personal brand may depend on how well you can impact the ideas, opinions and actions of others. An important way to increase your odds of influencing more people is to learn to recognize and use each of the five styles in business.

My influencer style as a personal brand is inspiring. Inspirers have the unique ability to energize and empower others. My personal mission is to inspire people to live their dreams through entrepreneurship. Through my coaching programs, trainings, and speeches, my goal is to equip people with the knowledge, tools, and confidence to become successful business owners.

> "There are times when you expect someone to be knowledgeable and good at what they do, and they meet or exceed your expectations. Then there are times when the conversation proves to change your scale. You realize that your expectations were not even close, and the scale was too small. That has been my experience with Tarsha. She is truly a professional at her chosen craft. Rarely are marketing professionals as adept at drawing out the right information so that they can truly understand you and your business. The time spent with Tarsha has me not only excited about my marketing strategy but has me even more passionate about the things that I love and do to help my clients."
>
> U. Metcalf
> Insured Liquidity Partners, LLC

Influencing Principles

Pushing is about selling, whereas pulling is about telling. To push, you need some kind of influence over the other person so that they make a shift. This is normally accomplished because you have that person's trust, or you have authority over things that they need.

In marketing, this can be seen when companies focus on a promotional strategy that pushes their products or services onto the customers. Have you ever walked down the grocery aisles and been approached by someone offering a sample of food? That is what is called a push strategy.

Pulling is accomplished by creating desire in the other person, working with what you know about what the other person wants, and understanding the way in which they will decide what they want. In marketing, the goal is to get customers to come to you by using engaging content, a referral program, telling stories that connect with your audience and advertising. When you use the influencing principal of a pull strategy you are creating loyal customers and repeat business.

Authority

We tend to believe people who are in positions of authority and trust, whether they have earned that trust or not. We trust doctors, police, and firefighters because we want to believe that they know what they are talking about; they yield more influence. Brands that have positioned themselves as the authority in their field have more influencing power.

Likability Factor

You already know that you will buy from or be convinced of something by people that you like. This is the likability factor. A known and likeable person can influence others. If it came down to a customer choosing between yours or your competitor's services when all options are equal, they most likely will choose to do business with the one they like the most.

Social Pressures

Oftentimes, we are influenced by what others have or what they are doing—it appeals to us. I was at a conference once and the woman next to me had this beautiful red briefcase. She told me it was purchased on Amazon. I took a picture of it and searched all over Amazon until I found that exact bag because what she had appealed to me. I was influenced by her and purchased the bag.

Self-Interests

Everything that we undertake includes some component of self-interest, and influencers are very conscious of this. To be self-interested means you seek your own personal gain. You use a push or pull marketing strategy because you want to attract customers to buy from you; in turn, you gain a profit. Why does a health insurance broker sell insurance? They want to make a living to provide for their own family. The agent offers affordable plans, a personal touch and great service. This convinces the customer to choose a plan. The agent is serving their self-interest, yet they offer something that would benefit the customer as well.

> *"Influence is powerful and subtle. You wouldn't let someone push you off course, but you might let someone nudge you off course and not even realize it."*
>
> *Jim Rohn*

Influencing through Communication

Influencing other people's behaviors requires carefully applied communication skills. You want to communicate for impact, with confidence and success.

Impactful communication focuses on the audience you are speaking to and tailoring your message to that audience. Pay attention to your choice of words, your tone, your tempo and whether the listener(s) understood. Plan what you have to say with intention so that your communication is clear and concise. If you start to ramble or use a lot of filler words such as, "um," "like," "so," your message might not resonate with the listener. You can have more influence when your communication has more substance and significance to the listener.

You can gain more of what you want and send stronger messages when you do so confidently. A business owner or leader who appears wishy-washy has no influence over their audience. The most confident people know who they are and understand how their level of confidence impacts others when communicating. Influencers who communicate with confidence demonstrate body language with an open and relaxed posture and minimal hand and body movements.

Influencers successfully use their interpersonal skills to inspire others to take action. Active listening involves listening with your eyes and ears while remaining quiet and clearing your mind of any thoughts you want to interject in the conversation. If you want to influence others to act on what you have to say, start by actively listening. Treat others with respect when communicating to establish trust. Once trust is established you can achieve your goal more effectively. Lastly, when you are masterful with your interpersonal skills you can control your emotions instead of being overwhelmed by them. This goes back to your tone. How your words come across can have an emotional impact. Focus on your facts not your feelings: 55% of communication is body language, 38% is tone and 7% is verbal. You can see how important communication is to someone wanting to become influential.

Influence and Assertiveness

Assertive is characterized by bold or confident statements and behavior. It is speaking up about your wants and needs while respecting the wants and needs of others. Assertive people:

- Know what they want and ask for it. As adults, we often struggle when it comes to asking for or accepting help. We can create future abundance in our lives just by mastering the art of asking assertively.

- Use I statements (I see, I think, I feel, I want, I will) to get their point across without sounding aggressive or passive. For example, "I feel strongly that it is time to move the company in another direction," instead of, "Maybe it's time to move the company in another direction."

- Stand out. They are not confused or offended when others see them as being different because of their level of confidence. People who are assertive influencers carry themselves with a confidence that others notice and are attracted to.

- Get others to listen by building rapport, matching and mirroring body language, and framing their message. Framing information means putting it into a context that helps audiences absorb and interpret it. How someone frames an issue influences how others see it or helps others focus their attention on particular aspects of it. For example, consider your team discussing how to improve a poor customer satisfaction rating. The conversation wanders from one point to another. Although discussion of each of these topics is fruitful, the team is not making much progress at finding a solution to the problem. This is where framing would be helpful.

You point out what is and isn't relevant to the issue at hand and bring the team back on track.

- Create what they want. They set concrete goals. They use influencing behaviors to achieve results and find resources they need to get what they want. Assertive influencers surround themselves with other influencers who can help them achieve their goals while making it beneficial to all.

Chapter Summary

You don't have to be a celebrity to be an influencer, but you do need to gain the qualities and skills that get people to listen and take action. The qualities and skills discussed in this chapter will help you promote yourself, build better relationships and leverage your influencer style to move the needle to where you want it to go.

Take some time and evaluate the influencing principals covered and determine which ones to incorporate in your personal brand. You'll be surprised how much more powerful your brand will become when you live by those principles.

Lastly, you might think popularity is what makes a person influential. While that is partly true, what makes a person influential is their ability to hone in on their interpersonal skills like communication, confidence and assertiveness.

Being an influencer is powerful. Building a personal brand that has influence is even more powerful.

Go to http://bit.ly/PBactionplan2 and download a personal brand action plan to help you dive deeper into building your powerful brand.

(How can you use the lessons in this chapter to increase your brand's influence? Use this page to write down your ideas and insights.)

CHAPTER FOUR

What's in a Name?

"Your brand is your name, basically. A lot of people
don't know that they need to build their brand;
your brand is what keeps you moving. "
Meek Mill

THOSE SIX YEARS I spent working in sales and marketing positions in the corporate world gave me helpful skills to start my own business and coach other entrepreneurs based on my experience. As a sales and marketing professional, I was doing the same things that my colleagues in the field were doing, and I found myself doing the same things my competition was doing as well.

The first name I had for my business was Pivotal Marketing Group. I wanted to create this marketing agency and offer the same or similar services as some of my competitors. There was nothing unique about what I did or what I offered. I struggled to differentiate myself. I eventually re-branded as The Marketing Lady and stopped offering services that I hated doing. Instead, I turned my marketing agency into a marketing coaching and consulting firm to focus on helping entrepreneurs become better marketers and developing marketing strategies that get results.

Creating a Great Brand Name

Every business needs a name that is memorable, describes its product or service, and conveys its expertise. As a business owner, select a business name that is best suited for your company's image and future growth. It should create a certain feeling when heard. When naming your company or personal brand, think about what impression prospective customers will have when they see the name on promotional materials, social media and advertisements. The name is the first thing a customer will see, and the first impression they get determines whether they will pick you over all the other companies in your category.

Creating a strong memorable business brand can help you stand out and get noticed. Before I rebranded my company to *The Marketing Lady*, people wouldn't remember my first or last name, but afterwards, they remembered my brand name. Why? Because it is memorable and stands out from the competition.

Be clear on what your brand represents and what you want your brand to mean to your target audience. There are some fundamentals involved when creating a business brand that will propel your product or service in the marketplace. In this next section, I will explain the steps you should take to create a powerful brand name.

Focus on the Business

Before even thinking of a brand, think of the nature of your business, the type of service to your customers and how you will be different from the competition. After all, the brand is merely a representation of your business. So, you must refrain from focusing too much on developing a brand that looks good without giving attention to the business itself. Your brand must be developed because of how you want to be perceived in the marketplace, not because of how the marketplace perceives your brand. I'll share this story to illustrate what I mean.

A few years ago, a hair stylist hired my firm to help her launch an online store that would carry a line of hair products that she private labeled. She wanted a brand that she would grow and one that would not be so dependent on her personal brand. Instead of using the name of the hair salon, we collaborated to create a business brand that was scalable online and offline. We got clear on the target audience her business would appeal to. She wanted her customers to feel they were getting luxury at an affordable price. Her hair collection came from places all over the world and she wanted to reflect that in the branding. Our team consulted her on her website, brand colors, logo, tag line, and core marketing messages. We successfully launched the Exotic Hair Collection inside of a small salon. A year and a half later, she called on my firm again. This time, she was expanding into a retail space. I was so proud of her success and to see her dream come true. Her business was growing, and her product line was expanding. We worked with her to do a grand opening launch with a local celebrity to create awareness about her new store and product.

"Tarsha has done an amazing job getting my business off the ground. She has created marketing materials and social media campaigns using Constant Contact to help brand my products.

Also, she has helped me with networking and coaching to form relationships with potential customers. In just a short time, I have seen real success with the growth of my business.

If you are looking for someone who is professional and can help you with all your marketing needs, then I highly recommend, Tarsha, The Marketing Lady to help you succeed!"

K. Browne
Owner/founder Exotic Hair Collection

Naming Strategy

A business name isn't only a name; it speaks to your brand identity. The business name helps customers associate what you do and builds your reputation. That is the reason most organizations spend and contribute most of their resources on building a brand that will increase the trust of its buyers, instead of going with names that literally describe the product. Go for something creative. However, having the product or service you offer in the name will be beneficial to your search results. For example, a search for a nail salon on Yelp or Google, one might type "nail salons" in the search bar. Hollywood Nail Spa might organically outrank MiniLux (these are actual nail salons) because the word "nail" is in the name. Another strategy might be to include your location in the name, if you are a locally based company that services a small geographical area. For example, Dallas European Auto not only includes the geographical location (which is great for local search results) but it also describes what it does. Catchy, creative names can be memorable even if they don't describe what the business does. For example, Dippin' Dots is both the product name (an ice cream snack) and the company name. There are many factors involved in naming your business or brand, such as the product/service features, how it will be used, and the benefits to the customer.

Brainstorm to Build a List

Brainstorm ideas with your business partners or advisors. Try to get into the minds of your target audience by identifying how your products or services meet their needs. While brainstorming, think of names that are easy to remember, describe your product, leave an impression, and have growth potential. Brainstorming names will bring out creativity and help you come up with a large selection from which to choose.

Use Online Tools to Narrow Your List

Use an online thesaurus to find all the synonyms for the words and phrases that you brainstormed. You can also use a keyword search tool to find a list of associated words. Make a list with different combinations of those words and pick ten to reflect upon. Share your list with people you trust and ask them for feedback. Narrow your list down to the three best choices and check trademarks, domain names, and with your local county clerk to learn if the names have been used. If you are not creative or you want to save some time, Shopify has a free business name generator tool you can use. Check it out on their website.[1]

Be Decisive

Pick the name that best encompasses everything your company stands for and is easy to remember. A business name is a valuable marketing tool, considering it is the first thing people know about your business. The name you choose is vital to the image of your brand and positioning of your company. So, choose wisely.

What Your Business Does

One naming strategy is based on what the product or service does. If you sell clothes, include that in the name. If you repair cars, include that in the name. You get the picture. If customers are confused about what you do and how you solve their problems, they won't do business with you. So, take time to evaluate what your business does and the distinct attributes and images it conveys in the marketplace. Who is your business catering to? What are their problems? What do you offer to solve their problems? By answering these questions will help establish the business brand.

Once you have established your brand purpose and business name, you are on your way to launching a powerful brand that will generate awareness of your products and services.

Chapter Summary

Creating a memorable business name or brand name is a marketing strategy companies use to increase awareness and stay top of the customer's mind. When you sneeze and need a tissue, you might say, "Hand me a Kleenex." Kleenex is a brand name that has become associated with tissue paper for the nose. A good name can help you with your online search results: it can make it easier to find you and can clearly explain what you do for the customer. A powerful brand needs a powerful name to be positioned for greatness.

Go to http://bit.ly/PBactionplan2 and download a personal brand action plan to help you dive deeper into building your powerful brand.

(How can you use the lessons in this chapter to create or improve your brand's naming strategy? Use this page to write down your ideas and insights.)

CHAPTER FIVE

Positioned for Greatness

"Success isn't always about greatness. It's about consistency.
Consistent hard work leads to success. Greatness will come."

Dwayne Johnson

A STRONG BRAND is built on its competitive position and how it communicates that position to its core audience. As you build your brand it's important to be cognizant of how your brand compares to other brands that sell what you sell to the audience you sell to. Competitive brand positioning is important because it establishes your competitive advantage and drives your business strategy.

Your competitive advantage is the favorable position you seek to be more profitable than your competition. To gain or even maintain this advantage, a company must differentiate itself in the marketplace. For example, Walmart is the number one retailer in the world because of its competitive advantage to offer "everyday low prices." [2] Therefore, its business strategy focuses on cost leadership. Walmart uses the everyday low prices philosophy in its marketing to its price-conscious audience.

So, what sets your brand and its products or services apart from competitors? What value do you provide and how is it different? You can position your brand for greatness by getting clear on your market profile, your target market segments, knowing how you deliver value to your customers and knowing your competition. My slogan is: *I Turn People into Brands®*. I came up with the tag line to sum up my promise of value to my customers.

Market Profile

Do research on the industry you are in and determine how large it is. A good place to start is your industry association. Is your market new, is it growing, maturing or declining? Here's an example. Remember a video store called Blockbuster? Blockbuster first opened its doors in the mid-1980s. I'm sure people were excited about the option of renting movies and taking them home instead of spending lots of money at the theater. At this point Blockbuster was in the introductory stage. As the trend to watch movies from home grew so did their profits, and ten years later, Blockbuster had 9,000 locations, was purchased by Viacom for $8.4 billion and went public on the stock market. Then, as Blockbuster matured, competitors like Netflix and Redbox entered the marketplace. Blockbuster tried to maintain its position in the marketplace by introducing a new product line, new features, and they launched major marketing campaigns. Unfortunately, one bad deal after another and the bad decision not to acquire Netflix for $50 million dollars accelerated their decline in subscribers by the year 2007. Sadly, by 2010, they filed for bankruptcy.[3] Today, there is only one Blockbuster store left located in Bend, Oregon.

Buyer Persona

Uncover the true needs and wants of your target market to make informed decisions on how to market to them. A buyer persona is a fictitious representation of your audience. It gives you an idea of who they are and what motivates them to buy what you offer. Knowing this will help you better understand how to position your brand in the minds of your audience. Creating a buyer persona requires some elbow grease. Pull your customer database, review website analytics, get insight from your sales team and staff who interact with customers. Interview customers and conduct surveys to gather all the data you need to create your persona. What's included?

- Basic demographic information (name, age, gender, location, income, education, and relationship status)
- Psychographics (lifestyle, interests, values, attitudes and behaviors)
- Challenges/fears

Buyer personas are wonderful to use when trying to establish competitive positioning. One of my clients owns a tax credits and incentives consulting company. The owner came to me because she wanted to differentiate her company among competitors and position herself as a thought leader in the field. After conducting research on the market, past and current customers, we came up with two fictitious characters. We'll focus on one for now.

Steve, The Expansion CEO

- CEO of a large, privately held manufacturing company with $10MM in annual revenue
- Located in the Midwest (demographic information).
- He wants to manage capital expenditures to achieve growth (goals).
- Steve is driven to succeed, extremely intelligent and skilled at negotiations (attitude/behavior).
- The challenge is that he has limited tax credits, incentives, and experience.
- He is in search of data that shows how firms that focus on tax credits and incentives have better outcomes when expanding (motivators).

With this customer profile and other information gathered, we came up with the buyer persona, Steve the Expansion CEO. Now the client is positioned to fill the knowledge gap and improve the bottom line for CEOs with expanding firms. My client's competitive position is to offer a partner-led approach to navigating the complex expansion and site relocation process. Steve is savvy, intelligent and knows how to negotiate well. All he needs is someone with experience in tax credits and incentives to guide him and his team through the process.

Information obtained through the buyer persona was used to create the content for the website, marketing communications strategy and even presentation topics for the owner.

"Before I started working with Tarsha as my personal brand coach, I did not have a fully developed personal brand, a strategy or plan in which to communicate my brand. During our monthly strategy sessions, I was able to learn more about my potential buyer, how to better position my brand and I gained insights about myself and my

firm's value-added services. As a result of working with Tarsha, I have a tailored brand communication plan with specific action items and insights I can implement immediately."

Julie Ashmore
President, Ashmore Consulting

Brand Value

The concepts surrounding a brand, such as a logo, tag line, mission statement, or color scheme are all fundamental to branding. What creates brand loyalty for your company and business is the experience that your customer has with your product or service. If your brand constantly delivers what it promises to customers, you will have loyal customers for life. It is essential to establish a relationship between your customer and the kind of service you bring to them. This one aspect will help you deliver value.

The perceived brand value of what you offer is a vital component to building a powerful brand. It is not merely about the image but addressing the emotional and physical needs of your customer to help reinforce your brand's market position. When your market can clearly see how what you offer is different from the competition, it's much easier to win market share.

A Brand that Knows the Competition

Many companies, even large ones, fail to do adequate market research before launching a new product or service. They pay little attention to their competition. If you cannot locate a competing business in your area, it means that there are some difficulties servicing the market locally or the demand is not great enough to be a feasible business. Conducting a competitive analysis will help you determine if there are firms that do what you do, or if there is a need for the services all together.

Determine How Many Local Competitors You Have

Start by going to the U.S. Census Bureau's website and looking up the NAICS code for your business type. A NAICS code is the standard used by the government in classifying business establishments. Once you have this number you can search the number of businesses in your metro area or county with the same code. This will give you a general number of how many companies provide similar services, but it will not tell you who they target. One of my favorite tools to use is *SizeUp* by the Small Business Administration.[4] It allows you to compare your business against local competitors, map your customers and determine where to target your advertising.

Research Their Website and Online Reviews

Next, research your competition by tracking and monitoring their websites and social media pages to find out how they are performing. There are many online tools that will allow you to compare your website traffic, see how your site ranks, and determine keywords audiences use to find your competitors. One of the best sites to use for this type of competitive analysis is Alexa.com. Also, research the online customer reviews of each of your competitors. *Google, Facebook* and *Yelp* are all great places to start your research. Websites like *Glassdoor* are also a great way to learn about a company from the employee perspective. Knowing what the competition is doing right and wrong, what they charge, and the quality of their services can help you in your business. Every company has strengths and weaknesses and by knowing your competition's, you can turn their weakness into your company's advantage.

Shop the Competition

If possible, have a friend or an employee patronize your competitions' businesses. They should call to get a quote or even become a customer. There is no better way to find out real information than to shop the competition. You will experience what they do, how they do it and the quality of their product or service. Plus, this will give you important information about their customer service, pricing, culture, and so on. My first internship in college was working for a retail consulting firm that conducted mystery shops for local shops. Part of my role was to go shop the competition. I had a set of criteria to evaluate and cash to purchase specific items. The information gathered was used to help the client analyze their competitor's strengths and weaknesses.

Join a Trade Organization

Finally, do some research using trade organizations in your field. You'll be surprised at the wealth of research data you can find from organizations that specialize in your field.

Competitive information is essential when starting any new business or expanding your brand's awareness. You can avoid several costly mistakes by doing your homework early on.

Chapter Summary

Learn about your customers and competition to position your brand as the top choice in the industry. Understand how your company compares to others in your market and stay on top of innovative trends. If possible, try to create your brand messaging specific to the target market you are aiming to reach. Use the buyer persona method to help segment your audience better. Becoming more customer centered instead of brand centered is important to building trust and rapport. Lastly, make sure you do some research on the competition using the tools mentioned. It will help you better understand your competitive advantage.

Go to http://bit.ly/PBactionplan2 and download a personal brand action plan to help you dive deeper into building your powerful brand.

(How can you use the lessons in this chapter to gain a competitive position? Use this page to write down your ideas and insights.)

PART 2

BUILD YOUR BRAND

"Always find a way to stand out from the crowd."

TARSHA POLK

CHAPTER SIX

I Have a Brand, Now What?

"Seize an opportunity to make a great impression."
Tarsha Polk

EVEN AFTER YOU have successfully crafted a brand name and image, getting noticed by your potential customers can be difficult when you have hundreds of competitors going after the same target audience. In the previous chapter, I told you how to research your competition and why that's important. In this chapter, I will show you how to get noticed.

Your customers are inundated daily with promotions via T.V., radio, social media, billboards, mailings, emails, people on the corner with signs, and the list goes on. So how do you compete with all the messages, images, and advertisements your customers are getting from competitors?

When I was coming up with a brand for my company, I knew it had to be unique and catchy so potential clients could remember me over the hundreds of marketing firms in the area. The Marketing Lady is simple yet effective! When people see my logo, hear my name, or experience one of my events, they think of marketing savvy, experience, and a company that walks the talk with great networking events. Your goal is to create a way to stand out from the crowd, so read on.

Stand Out from the Crowd

Jay Abraham, father of Guerrilla Marketing said, "Whenever a customer needs the type of product or service you sell, your USP should bring your company immediately to mind." What's unique about your brand that makes you better than the competition and will convince customers to switch brands? To answer this question, you need to create a unique selling proposition (USP). Your USP gives you the competitive edge. It tells what you can promise or guarantee that is different from your competition. You should be able to explain your company's uniqueness in one simple statement, and you must be able to fulfill the promise you make in that statement. Your prospective customers may have a hard time deciding which company to buy from so why not make it easy for them to choose you?

1. What benefit is unique to your offering, and what is the basis of this claim? This is what you offer that no one else does in your market. Maybe it's a unique way in which you season your food, the technology you have, or it could be your customer service that makes you unique. Take some time to list all the unique benefits of your offering. If you can't find anything unique about it, look back at your competitive analysis to see how you can differentiate yourself.

2. Who is the target market for whom this benefit is of compelling interest? Knowing why your audience

would buy what you sell is critical to establishing your USP. What problem are you solving? What need are you meeting? Take some time to list what you know about your target audience and how your product/services meet their needs.

3. How is your USP different or better than your competitors? Review your competitive analysis to determine what you do that your competition can't duplicate or beat. Netflix was able to be different and better than Blockbuster with its USP, "Watch Anywhere. Cancel Anytime." Technology is what they used to differentiate themselves.

If you struggle with defining your USP, you'll have a hard time convincing the customer to buy from you. Here are a few examples to give you a better idea of what a good USP sounds like.

The Marketing Lady's USP: Delivering value and creating synergistic relationships.

FedEx: When it absolutely, positively has to be there overnight.

Target: Expect More. Pay Less.

You are probably thinking a USP is just a slogan, and it can be used that way. A USP is a way to position and sell your product as a part of your marketing strategy.

I'm the first to admit it is a challenge to get noticed among thousands of marketing coaches! Once you find your uniqueness, your competition quickly duplicates what you do or offer, making it hard to be different. Earl Graves Sr., founder of *Black Enterprise* once said, "In business, true opportunities are scarce, obstacles are many and success demands being prepared for both." Getting noticed among thousands of people who are going after the same things can be difficult. You can make sure that you stand out from the crowd by going above and beyond when an opportunity presents itself. A perfect example comes to mind.

When Super Bowl XLV came to North Texas, one year prior to the actual game, the NFL worked with local businesses, community leaders, former NFL players and local influencers to form the North Texas Super Bowl Host Committee. The role of the committee was to create awareness and facilitate the available opportunities to do business with the NFL during Super Bowl XLV. The committee hosted several workshops and events to expose local business owners to those opportunities. I attended a few sessions held at Cowboy Stadium in Arlington, TX. There were a few thousand business owners at one event I attended. I must say, I felt intimidated by the large number of marketing/advertising firms listed in the vendor guide. There were over 200 marketing firms listed, all competing for a contract with the NFL.

During the program I thought there was no way I could compete with some of the bigger marketing firms. I felt hopeless, sitting in the center of the auditorium surrounded by my competitors and other small businesses. I didn't think I would ever get noticed or even selected as a vendor to do business with the NFL. Suddenly, one of my mother's sayings came to mind, "You can do anything you set your mind to." That's when I had an idea on how I could stand out and get noticed.

One of the North Texas Host committee members stated they needed more people to be aware of their Emerging Business

Program. At the time, I produced and hosted an Internet talk radio show called, *Let's Talk Success with The Marketing Lady.*[5] I believed that having them as a guest on my show would not only benefit them, but me as well. After the presentation was over, I fought my way through the crowd of people (I was sitting in the center) to make my way upfront. While most people gravitated towards the high-profile people to shake hands and get pictures, I targeted the director of the host committee. I introduced myself and briefly told her about my Internet radio show. I gave her my card and suggested she be a guest to create more awareness about the program. After a couple of months of nurturing the relationship and following up, the director agreed to be a guest on the show. It was one of my most listened to shows that year. You can listen to the interview here: http://bit.ly/superbowl45NTX.[6]

I quickly seized the opportunity to make a great impression, help solve their problem and stand out. Through this connection, I was later offered a contract to do business with the NFL. I'll tell you more about this in a later chapter.

Going above and beyond is a key ingredient to successfully getting noticed in a highly competitive environment. Opportunities like this are not as scarce as you might think. If you look at your network, for example, you're sure to find someone that you could genuinely help by going above and beyond what others are willing to do.

So how do you compete with all the messages, images, and advertisements your customers are getting from competitors? You must position your brand to get people to start talking about you, thinking about you, and spreading the word about you. The buzz (publicity) I received from the Super Bowl continues to bring me referrals and keeps my company top of mind.

Remember, when you are creating buzz, you are attaching your unique selling proposition to a product, service, or expertise. You are promoting the fact that you can deliver an experience better than anyone else. Make your brand stand out by:

- Having memorable marketing messages.
- Having a recognizable brand identity such as your logo, symbol or personal image.
- Being authentic.
- Having eye-catching social media and website images and headlines.
- Posting relevant and targeted content on social media.
- Networking with purpose.
- Exuding confidence.
- Doing something inspirational.
- Sharing your story.
- Focusing on building relationships.
- Giving more than you expect to receive.

Other ways to promote your brand are through company accomplishments and success stories you can share which will help to establish creditability and showcase your expertise. Here are a few "stand out" success stories from clients.

> ### Case Study: Valerie's Pickles
>
> *Valerie launched a line of flavored pickles.*
>
> *Our Advice: Create a mascot similar to the Planter's peanut for her brand to be more recognizable.*
>
> *Action: Valerie created a costumed mascot so that when she attended trade show events her brand would "Stand out from the Crowd."*

Result: Valerie attracted attention from the media and has been in the Dallas Morning News, on radio, T.V. and attracted the attention of one of Oprah's producers during a broadcast from the State Fair of Texas.

Case Study: Janeva's Concierge Services

JCS was a start-up virtual assistance and errand service for small business owners. The owner launched this business her senior year in college with guidance from The Marketing Lady. Instead of getting a job out of college, she wanted to be self-employed. The challenge was she had no experience running a business nor did she know how to obtain clients.

Our Advice: Establish a brand that is focused on local entrepreneurs where she can build personal relationships and focus on high-level customer service. Doing this would separate her business from competitors whose online services provide no personal touch. Network with local business associations and groups to form relationships.

Result: Through the networking strategy coaching, she was able to secure her first client within 30 days of launching.

Chapter Summary

The important thing to learn from this chapter is creating your unique selling proposition and how to use it to stand out. Use some of the techniques mentioned to help you attract more clients and opportunities. Brainstorm ideas on how you can stand out from your competition, even if that means reinventing yourself. I hope the story I shared about my NFL experience will inspire you to take a different approach to how you market your brand.

Go to http://bit.ly/PBactionplan2 and download a personal brand action plan to help you dive deeper into building your powerful brand.

(How can you use the lessons in this chapter to stand out and get noticed? Use this page to write down your ideas and insights.)

CHAPTER SEVEN

Boost Your Social Visibility

"The power of visibility can never be underestimated."
Margaret Cho

TRADITIONAL MARKETING IS still a great way to gain new clients. However, increasing your social visibility should be your top priority if you are to stand out and get noticed. One of the greatest benefits of social media is turning people into brand evangelists when they talk about your brand online in addition to the added visibility. When you post engaging content, interact with your followers and follow other influencers on social media, you get discovered and you can generate new business.

I used social media and other online platforms to create awareness and build my brand locally and internationally. Although I have a Dallas/Ft. Worth based firm, I have an international brand thanks to social media. According to recent social media insights, my Facebook social followers are in nine other countries: Canada, United Kingdom, Nigeria, India, Pakistan,

Japan, Germany, Egypt, and Benin. My Twitter followers are in Canada, United Kingdom, Australia, India, Philippines, Indonesia, Netherlands, Italy, and Germany.

I wanted to use social media to position my brand as an expert and to generate leads. The strategy you use depends on your goals and industry you are in. For example, if you are an online retailer, you'd want to sell products directly through Facebook and advertise on it as well. You can use the Facebook set up shop feature on your business page to add and sell your product.[7] Or, you can use 3rd party e-commerce platforms like Shopify to integrate your online store with Facebook.

Effective Use of Social Sites

- Brand Consistency. Make sure your brand image is consistent across all social platforms so that you're easily recognized. Be sure you get a vanity URL for all of your social media pages. A vanity URL looks like this: www.facebook.com/yourbrandname.
  My vanity URL for Facebook is www.facebook.com/themarketinglady. Not only does it help to identify your company on the social platform, it also improves your searchability.

- Brand Visibility. Build your audience by joining group discussions, writing sharable content, engaging followers by inviting conversation, providing informative, useful content and incentives. The more you engage with social followers the more visibility you have in their newsfeeds and timelines. This increases your exposure well past the number of followers you have. Creating your own group is also an effective use of social media.

The benefit here is that you get to control the content and build your own tribe of interested followers who want to hear what you have to say.

- Audience Engagement. Post pictures and videos to get more people engaged with your pages and to increase your reach. Videos get more engagement than just text alone. Live video outperforms uploaded video. According to a report from Facebook, 1 in 5 videos on Facebook is a live broadcast.[8]

- Search Engine Ranking. Social media helps with your search engine ranking. When you type in a brand's name, their social pages are usually on the first page. This means you'd want to make sure you optimize your social media profiles by using keywords/phrases in the about section, bio, and use hashtags to help people find you. Use effective call-to-actions to drive social media followers to your website. In marketing, a call-to-action is a word or phrase that entices the viewer, listener, or reader to perform a specific act. An example of a call-to-action are words like "click here, buy now, download." You can do this by posting content from your website blog, posting a link to a landing page or including a link to your website for visitors to learn more.

- Targeted Advertising. For a small fee, you can create ads that target by age, gender, location, interests and other demographics. Remember the client who launched a new line of hair products? The marketing strategy we developed included spending $5 - $20 a month to reach 1,500 to 2,000 women over age 25. By investing a small amount of money each month, she has been able to increase traffic to her online store and grow her fans. This is a very affordable way to get exposure and drive traffic to your website or social pages.

- Lead Generation. If done correctly and frequently, you can build a strong opt-in email list using social media. Capture emails from social media to get leads into your sales funnel and market to them. LinkedIn, Facebook, Instagram, and Twitter all have paid lead generation advertising features. Before I started investing in Facebook Ads to build my list, I would promote an event on my pages. In each post, a link to RSVP was included, which allowed me to capture emails.

Become a Social Influencer

You can become a social media influencer by nurturing and growing an online community of people who respect your opinions and find the information you share impactful. When you become a social influencer, you will have brand evangelist who will do the marketing for you by sharing your information on their platforms. Influencers can influence buying decisions simply by reviewing a product, sharing their experience with a service or product, writing about a product or service or simply promoting it.

To become a social media influencer, pick a subject area to focus on. This could be something you are good at, a passion of yours, or your everyday routine. Once you've figured out what to focus on, then pick 1 – 2 social channels best for your content and then dominate. For example, perhaps you want to become a lifestyle influencer and share your love for bikes and riding.

LinkedIn wouldn't be the best platform, but Instagram and Facebook would.

Build your followers by posting authentic, yet engaging content and use trending hashtags like #FollowBack. Engage with your followers and contribute value to other community groups and profiles you follow. As a rule of thumb, content can fall into these three categories: fun and entertaining, informative, and promotional. Let's use the example about the lifestyle influencer. Since this person has a passion for riding bikes, their content can be a mix of informative (how to select the right bike) and entertaining (videos or pictures of scenes from their riding adventures).

Connect with other social influencers. Influencers have thousands of followers on multiple platforms and high engagement. This is a great way to grow your reputation and build credibility by collaborating with them on a campaign. Build a relationship with them before pitching to them to share your online content. Try to get an introduction by one of their connections. Comment on their posts and share something they posted. Interview them in your blog, on your podcast or webinar to create a win-win relationship.

Keep in mind that some influencers want a fee to help promote your brand to their loyal base of followers, and rightly so. Many influencers spend long hours providing content and work hard to grow their fan base. According to an article on Bufferapp.com, a known social media management tool, influencers are paid based on the number of followers or engagement. The article states that Instagram influencers might receive $10 per 1,000 followers or $250 - $750 per 1,000 engagements.[9] So, it's easy to understand why influencers want a fee.

Host a Podcast

For three years, I hosted *Let's Talk Success*, an Internet talk radio show on BlogTalk Radio. My first live podcast aired online February 23, 2008. That show received 769 unique listens. I chose that platform because it had a built-in audience that would be exposed to my brand.

I did a 30 – 45-minute show every week. My show averaged 300 listeners and downloads. My archived shows are still running on the site (www.blogtalkradio.com/letstalksuccess) and my brand continues to gain exposure to over 100,000 listeners in the U.S. and internationally (see chart below). Not only will you gain exposure, but podcasts help to establish your credibility. Podcasts are also great platforms to educate and inform. Get your podcast on some of the popular platforms to help you gain exposure. Some podcast platforms to consider are BlogTalk Radio, Apple Podcast, Simplecast, Soundcloud and Libsyn. All you need to get started is a good microphone and headset. Podcast hosting services allow you to record and store the content you will ultimately distribute in your podcast. Many of them have free options so it is an affordable way to stand out and get noticed.

Country	Share
United States	79.54%
India	6.81%
Nigeria	20.93%
New Zealand	6.66%
Australia	1.92%

Figure 1
Audience Geography

Blogging

Several years ago, every business was starting a blog. It was essential to create a good one to promote your business and improve your ranking with search engines. With Facebook and LinkedIn (all sites from which you can blog), blogs have had to adapt to stay on people's minds and remain relevant. Blogging today is not what it was a few years ago. Companies started blogs so they would have fresh content on their websites to help drive traffic and keep repeat visitors. Now, video content is attracting larger audiences than the long-form content of a blog post.

People have short attention spans equal to or shorter than a Goldfish; consequently, one of the key things to remember about blogging is to keep your blog posts short. Seth Godin, who writes about marketing and has a brilliant blog, sometimes creates posts that are only a few hundred words long. Whether you are creating short, informative pieces that are less than 500 words, or longer, more introspective pieces, you want people to read, remember, and think about your blog.

I suggest that you frequently create content that will be interesting to your audience and post it on your blog weekly. Content can come in many forms: video, pictures, interviews and infographics. Develop a list of keywords and use them strategically throughout your blog posts because every post that you create is like creating a web page that is rich with keywords. A blog that's linked to your website helps with organic reach in search engines and increases your rankings.

Another way to promote your business through blogging is to become a guest blogger on someone else's site. People are always looking for content ideas. Connect with a blogger who targets the same audience and form a relationship. If they have a lot of subscribers, you'll increase your exposure. You can also create traffic by posting a link on your Facebook page, LinkedIn page, or on Twitter to broaden your audience.

Vlog

If writing is not your thing, create a vlog (a blog in video format) and do a weekly Facebook Live or YouTube channel to distribute your content. The more you stand out with your brand name, image and message, the more you will attract new clients and new opportunities.

Social Media Success Strategy

Boosting your social visibility requires you to have a strategy. You need to have a strategy for how to leverage social media because individuals have embraced it as a part of everyday life. Social media is one element within your overall marketing mix. Just like with any strategy you develop, you must start with the goals and objectives you want to accomplish.

For example, your objective might be to drive traffic to your brick and mortar storefront. So, your goal might be to increase traffic by 10% in a given month. Your strategy then is to use Facebook ads to advertise in-store promotions during that month. Your ad will run for 30 days with the message, "Have a Cup of Joe on Me. Buy-1, Get-1 Free! Mention FreeJoe at our stores."

Although it is free to use social media, you'll still want to create a budget. Your budget would include things like any advertising fees you will incur, graphic design fees for the ads, salary of the social media manager and any promotions you will run. Outline the amount per month for each category and then calculate the approximate ROI (return on investment) and set time frame (months/years). The costs are generally easier to track in social media marketing than revenues are so use tracking pixels to track a website visitor's behavior and conversion. A tracking pixel is a snippet of code that is loaded when a visitor goes to a website or opens an email. Be conscientious about your budget because social media is easy to use and can also be very time consuming.

Chapter Summary

The main benefit of boosting your social media visibility is to increase your brand awareness to a built-in audience already using the platform. When you develop your social media strategy, don't forget to leverage the various lead generation features that will allow you to capture email addresses and other information, so you can remarket to them. Use social media to build your customer relationships and brand loyalty. And finally, use it to drive traffic to your website.

Go to http://bit.ly/PBactionplan2 and download a personal brand action plan to help you dive deeper into building your powerful brand.

(How can you use the lessons in this chapter to increase your social visibility? Use this page to write down your ideas and insights.)

CHAPTER EIGHT

But I Don't Know How to Network

*"Understand the power of networking and
how it can increase your influence and drive sales."*
Tarsha Polk

ETWORKING IS A powerful marketing strategy to acceler-
ate and sustain success for any individual or business. Your
ability to connect with people is essential to developing profitable relationships. Need more clients, more referrals and more
sales? Then, networking should be in your marketing strategy.
Whether you've been in business for 6 months or 16 years,
networking with potential customers is significant to your marketing strategy. However, many small business owners, marketers
and sales people still do not understand the power of networking and how it can increase their influence and drive sales.

I mentioned in chapter two that my networking journey started out as networking for a job, which turned into networking to grow my own business. Now, you would think that someone with sales experience and a degree in marketing would be pretty good at networking, right? Wrong! I was networking every day and returning home feeling like I wasted my time because I didn't get qualified leads. I'm sure you can probably relate to this; can't you? If you are an introvert, it may be difficult for you to make connections that will help you succeed in business and life. You don't have to be very outgoing to succeed, but if you are in a position where you need to meet new people and network with strangers you might feel a little bit uncomfortable.

How to Network

Networking is expanding your social network or sphere of influence by initiating mutually beneficial relationships with people. During in person networking, learning the art of mingling can lead you to your ideal customer. It is best to move freely about the crowd in a social or business setting, so you can get to know the right people who might be potential clients or referral sources. If you are an introvert, you are less likely to mingle. You may smile, nod your head and converse with those who walk by or approach you, but that's not mingling. Try to approach individuals instead of a group of people because it may be hard to break the circle of a group. Go to a networking event with a "wing man," so you can feel more relaxed about approaching people.

Focus your time on building rapport so you can schedule a meeting for a one-on-one later to establish a relationship.

Building rapport takes confidence, active listening skills and the ability to establish trust.

- Learn about the other person first. This gives you a chance to learn how what you offer might help them.
- Find something you have in common with them. This will give you more to talk about and helps to establish trust.
- Show genuine interest in the person by listening and sharing feedback or resources that can help them.
- Be positive with your tone, body language and overall attitude.

Businesses runs on relationships. As a business owner, you must form relationships with customers, investors, suppliers and employees. There is a limited amount of time to build relationships at a networking event, but if you meet a prospect that you'd like to establish a relationship with, invest quality time with them.

I used to be a bit shy, until I graduated college and got a job in sales. I had no idea what networking really was nor did I know that the position would require me to do a lot of it. Because I wanted to succeed in the job, I had to make the necessary adjustments and overcome the anxiety of meeting new people.

The first thing I did was observe how other individuals interacted in business networking settings. I attended an event with a colleague who was an excellent networker. She knew how to generate leads, so I shadowed her whenever I could. My observations helped me figure out how to approach people and what conversations to start.

Whether you are an introvert or extrovert, there are a few things I recommend avoiding while networking.

Bad Networking Habits

- Don't be a wallflower. Remember your high school dance? Do you remember seeing kids holding up the wall instead of being out on the dance floor or socializing with the other kids? Even today, adults who are introverted will stand off in the corner or hold up the wall waiting for someone to come talk to them. Well, let me tell you, you're not in high school anymore and a prospect is not coming to you—you must go after them!

#Networking Hack: Ask the first person you meet to introduce you to someone they met. This will get you off the wall and mingling.

- Avoid talking more than you listen. When we are in sales mode, we are so focused on talking about our products, services or even ourselves that we fail to listen effectively to the other individual. Listening is a skill. It is different from hearing. When you listen, you are processing the information you heard to understand the person. A skillful listener listens to understand and not to respond.

#Networking Hack: Listen to understand the other person's needs or problems/issues. Listen for rapport building clues so you can establish a connection with them. Listen to determine if they are a prospect for you.

- Avoid making the conversation mostly about you and your company. Networking is about the mutual exchange of information, resources and connections. How could you possibly get to know the person you are talking to and their needs if you dominate the conversation by making it about you? Be sure to ask open ended questions like, how can I help you? What type of contact or referral are you looking for? These types of questions will get them talking about their own business and what they may need. Other questions to ask are: what would you like to accomplish at today's event? Is there anyone I can introduce you to?

#Networking Hack: Work to build rapport and show the other person that it's all about him or her.

- Don't just pass out business cards to people without making a connection with the person first. What I mean by connection is that you have identified something you have in common with them or they have seriously expressed a need for your services.

#Networking Hack: Prove to your prospects that you can fulfill their business needs. Even if a connection is not made right away, find out what types of clients they need. Who knows? You might have a referral for them.

I made many of these mistakes during the early stages of my business. I was frustrated with the poor results I was getting from my networking efforts and the stack of business cards that didn't convert to clients. Then one day I decided to jot down all the things I was doing right and wrong and developed a networking plan. I promise you that if you do the same, you will see tremendous results from your efforts as well.

Chapter Summary

Getting together with other businesspeople for the mutual purpose of increasing visibility and advocating referrals is the backbone of networking and it can be beneficial to promoting your business. However, most people don't know how to network effectively. Overcome your networking fears and avoid some of the most common mistakes people make when networking. Surprisingly, one of those mistakes is that most people don't develop a networking strategy.

Move beyond the business card to strategic networking for success and learn techniques to incorporate networking into your overall marketing strategy. In the next chapter, I'll teach you seven steps you can take to develop your very own strategic networking plan.

Go to http://bit.ly/PBactionplan2 and download a personal brand action plan to help you dive deeper into building your powerful brand.

(How can you use the lessons in this chapter to become a better net-worker? Use this page to write down your ideas and insights.)

PART 3

REDEFINE YOUR BRAND

---

*"I feel like I have a job to do, like
I constantly have to reinvent myself. The
more I up the ante for myself, the better it
is in the long run."*

KEVIN HART

CHAPTER NINE

7 Steps to Networking Success

"Networking is an essential part of building wealth."
Armstrong Williams

IN THIS CHAPTER, I will show you how to power up your networking and maximize your success by creating a seven-step networking strategy. Strategy is defined as a plan, method, or series of maneuvers for obtaining a specific goal or result. You must focus on the process of defining goals and objectives and then develop activities to reach those goals and objectives.

Step 1: Identify Your Target Audience

Before you can start networking for business or career, you must first identify your target market. Your target audience is simply the people who will most likely buy your products and/or services. In chapter four, I discussed how to segment your audience based on basic demographic information.

Knowing this basic information about your audience will help you better locate them and identify networking opportunities.

Before developing your networking strategy, study your target audience and list five reasons why they would buy your product or services. These five reasons should be related to how you solve their problems or help them overcome a challenge. Next, list the features and benefits of what you offer. You must clearly understand what features and benefits to offer your target audience to know how to effectively network and market to them.

> *Feature: A feature is a basic part or quality of your product or service.*
>
> *Benefit: An advantage your product or service has to offer.*

Let's say you are a wellness coach who offers nutritional meal plans, health assessments, and one-on-one support to individuals who want to live a healthy lifestyle. A feature of your service could be an app where clients can track their eating habits and activities. The benefit of that app is the convenience of having instant access to the information needed to stay on track with their eating habits.

Step 2: Determine Your Networking Goals

Strategic networking will save you time and money if you create a plan. The next thing you'll need to do is determine what your networking goals are. Are you networking to develop relationships, generate leads, business development, etc.? This is important for helping you determine what type of networking organization to join or event to attend.

Establishing goals will give you a better idea of what networking situations to get involved in and eliminates wasting your time. S.M.A.R.T. goals help you clearly state what you want, where you want to be, who you want to work with, and what you will need to make it happen. S.M.A.R.T. goals are:

- Specific – They describe the details of what you want out of each networking situation. Know the "who, what, when, where, and how" of your goal.
- Measurable – Each goal you establish should be quantifiable. It helps you measure whether you have obtained the number you are trying to reach.
- Achievable – Your networking goals must be important to you and you must be committed to working hard to achieve them.
- Realistic – Is the goal you created doable based on your skills, capabilities, resources, and time? Can you really talk to 100 people at every networking event you attend?
- Timely – Each goal you set should have a timeframe within which it should be accomplished; otherwise, you will not push yourself to achieve the goal.

The following example will help you set your S.M.A.R.T. goals. Let's say that you want to obtain ten qualified leads to schedule one-on-one appointments with you in the next 30 days. A few typical networking goals include:

- Develop relationships with referral partners

- Generate leads
- Increase sales
- Gain professional development
- Meet new and influential people
- Build credibility
- Increase awareness about product/service

Step 3: Find the Right Networking Opportunities

Remember in chapter four I talked about how I attended a workshop put on by the NFL and the North Texas Host Committee? I attended their Emerging Business workshop with the goal of making a connection with the key decision makers who could hire my company to do work for the NFL. This session had all the major decision makers attending as well as people who would influence the decision makers. With proper planning and preparation, I was in the right networking opportunity at the right time.

I realize that finding the best networking events can be difficult. Strategic networking involves planning—planning which events, seminars, meetings, or organizations you want to be involved in. If you have not attended an organization or meeting before, do some research using the Internet, trade publications or member directories. Learn whether your target market will be represented during such events. Make note of the information you have gathered and use it to your advantage. Visit the organization's website to find an online directory of its members and leaders. The more you know the better you can determine if you've found the right networking opportunity.

For example, let's say you have recently opened a children's activity center. Go to www.meetup.com to find a "stay at home mom" group to network with. Learn how many members and/or attendees go to meetings. Check off the members you would like to meet or do business with and strategize your initial introduction.

Find out who the centers of influence are in the group. The center of influence is the person(s) most respected or listened to in the group. They can be the group creator or meeting organizer. This person usually knows everyone and can influence how decisions are made. The center of influence at the NFL event I attended was the director of the North Texas Host Committee. She had direct contact and interactions with buyers of goods/services and those in charge of the Emerging Business Program. I found out more about her by looking in the event program book. I introduced myself to her. I figured if I could build rapport with her, I'd get exposed to opportunities to do business with the NFL. Later I'll share with you how I was able to leverage my network of influential people who may have impacted the Director's and NFL program manager's decision to reach out to me for a contract.

Social Media Networking Opportunities

Hands down, LinkedIn is the best networking tool for business-to-business professionals. Most people who utilize LinkedIn do so for three primary reasons:

1. They want to do business.
2. They are looking for a career.
3. They are promoting their personal brand.

Use LinkedIn to make real connections by connecting with people you know and those who will engage with your posts.

Connect with people in the business community and give a brief introduction when requesting or accepting a connection request. Join groups your prospects are in and contribute value-added comments to existing group conversations. Build trust with your connections by focusing more on them and less on you. If you come across like a used car salesman, it is likely your social network won't engage with you. Search for and target prospects for the purpose of building relationships, sharing resources and making comments on their posts. You can use LinkedIn search features to find your ideal prospect.

Another social media platform that is good for networking is Facebook. I find networking within Facebook groups to be very effective. Just like LinkedIn, people join social media groups on Facebook to connect with individuals with similar interests. There are groups that allow you to promote what you do or promote an event; however, avoid being spammy. It is better to share useful links, start a relevant discussion and answer questions.

Use Facebook groups to build brand credibility by constantly being present and offering up helpful information. It's okay to post about your company when the situation calls for it. For example, in a peer group I am in, someone posted they wanted a recommendation for a brand coach. I simply responded with a link to my website and explained how I worked with clients. Best practices for networking in Facebook groups:

- Ask questions or conduct a poll that is centered around the problems your audience usually faces. For example, if you are a realtor, create a poll that says, "When looking for a home, the most important factors are (a) school district, (b) location to work, (c) number of bedrooms."

- Make sure you are aware of the group rules before posting. Violating the rules may get you kicked out of the group.
- Join the group of your ideal audience. If you are a CPA, join a group for startup firms. Share helpful tips to keep your brand top of mind.

Facebook is great for getting your name out there and landing new clients. If you don't have a business page, create a personal page and use it for networking purposes. Complete your personal profile to include your company, its website, work experience and your job title. This information can be added in the "About Section" of your profile and a short elevator pitch or brand statement in the "Intro Section." People will be able to hover over your profile and find out who you are and what you do.

In-person networking is being overshadowed by social networking to expand one's network. In 2009, I planned a trip to London for vacation. I decided to go to Meetup.com to see what networking groups I might want to visit while there. I connected with a group called *Stiletto Millionaires*. I introduced myself to the coordinator and asked about upcoming events. A few weeks later, she invited me to their June mixer. A few weeks after that, she asked me to be their June speaker. I used social media to network my way into my very first international speaking engagement.[10]

Build a Tribe

While I do encourage you to create a business page for your brand, I also recommend creating your own group page for networking purposes. Start your own tribe or community of people who are dissatisfied with something or whose needs are not being met. On a group page there are more available features to engage with your tribe than there are on a business page, such as: group chat, file sharing, and messaging. The benefit of starting your own community is that you can connect with your ideal audience in a more personal way and better control how you promote your professional brand.

Step 4: Create a Magnetic Elevator Pitch that Piques Interest

Do you have a compelling elevator pitch? Now that you've determined your goals and identified your networking opportunities, it's time to develop your marketing message and any marketing collateral you may need for the event. Your verbal marketing message or "elevator pitch" is a short 30-second answer to "What do you do?" In those 30 seconds, you should state how your product or service will benefit your customer or solve a problem.

Answer these questions:

- What does the business do?
- Who do you do it for?
- What do they want or what can you offer?
- How does your business solve a problem or offer a solution?
- What makes your business unique?

An Examination of My Pitch

My name is Tarsha Polk, The Marketing Lady. I turn people into brands. (*This statement answers the question: What does the business do?*) I help entrepreneurs build influential brands that attracts more clients and opportunities by creating a marketing framework that works. (*This statement answers another question: Who do you do it for? It also states how my business solves a problem.*)

After I give my pitch, most people ask, "How do you turn people into brands?" This lets me know I've piqued their interest. I tell them I'm a personal brand strategist and marketing consultant. I help my clients figure out what makes them or their service unique and then I create a marketing campaign around that. The goal of your elevator pitch is to get your ideal audience asking questions and requesting more information about your services.

> "*Networking success is inevitable when you leverage your local network and turn contacts into contracts.*"
>
> Tarsha Polk
> The Marketing Lady

Step 5: Mingle to Work the Room

You will encounter four different types of networking personalities while you are mingling with others. Which one are you? Find your type and use the tip.

> **Owl** - *Individuals who prefer to work alone and who are often not at ease in social situations. These are your wallflowers; they watch everyone and wait for others to come talk to them. They network occasionally because they need to.*
>
> **Tip:** *Ask to be introduced to others by people you meet. Take baby steps and initiate introducing yourself to three people.*
>
> **Otter** - *Otters are very social creatures. Otter personalities love people. They enjoy being popular and influencing and motivating others. These are the people you see working the room and talking*

to everyone. Otters love talking. Be cautious of how much talking you do versus listening to the other person while networking.

Tip: Ask 1 - 2 questions that will get the other person talking about themselves or their business.

<u>Lion</u> - The King/Queen of the networking event. They are persuasive leaders and incredibly powerful people. They are well connected, have strong business relationships and will connect with you for a common purpose that benefits all. They may dominate the networking situations or become frustrated when their time is wasted.

Tip: Be aware when you are dominating the conversation and allow time for others to speak. Pay close attention to your body language to ensure it is open and inviting.

<u>Beaver</u> - Beavers are organized and like to take a practical approach to things. They network with intention. They are consistent with their actions, follow up when they meet people, see opportunities, and connect people. They understand the true value of networking. Importantly, they plan their business networking activities. Beavers can be so focused on their plan/goal that they do little socializing while networking.

Tip: Put people before the plan. Build rapport!

Knowing your networking personality and that of those in the room will help you to better communicate and make connections.

If your goal for attending the event is to prospect for new business, ask the host or event organizer if they can introduce you to someone who fits your ideal client. Once introduced, have casual conversation until you've determined that the person is a good contact and ask what they do. Most likely the person will ask the same. A word of caution that bears repeating: Do not act like a used car salesman and try to sell them during the entire conversation. No one likes a pushy sales presentation.

At networking events or social settings, you don't know if a person is a good prospect unless you ask qualifying questions. Carefully choose qualifying questions to uncover the individual's needs as they relate to what you offer. Ask open-ended questions to keep them talking. A marketing person might ask, "What results do you get from your marketing efforts?" An insurance representative might ask, "What are your biggest concerns regarding protecting your family?" A travel agent might ask, "How would you benefit from an affordable getaway?"

The goal is to find out if they are ready, willing, and able to purchase what you have. Remember, you are not giving a sales presentation, so be conversational with your questions. Schedule a phone or in-person meeting if they seem interested in learning more.

Use these tips to get the most out of every situation where you are networking.

Step 6: Turn Contacts into Contracts

Have you ever scrolled through your contacts on your cell phone or contact management tool to see hundreds of names and numbers you don't even call? Or maybe you have a binder full of business cards you collected from networking events. Do you know that direct marketing firms would kill for the contacts you have right at your fingertips? Failure to utilize your personal and business contacts causes you to miss out on opportunities!

However, once you have a simple and effective strategy put together, it will be easier to turn your contacts into contracts. As you go through your contacts, answer these questions:

1. Is there anyone in your existing network that can support you?
2. Who are the five people you met through networking that you will reconnect with in the next 30 days?

Speaking of the people you have access to, do you know how much your network is worth? Jim Rohn, a motivational speaker, has been credited with saying, "You are the average of the five people you spend the most time with." Your five closet friends determine your revenue. If you want to increase your average, you must increase your net worth and network 50% more. Network with high potentials who have a common interest with you like a member of your church, community leaders, a neighbor or someone who provides services to you. When you have identified the high net worth network, there are a few things you must do.

High Net Worth Network

- Educate them on what you do and who you target.
- Make it easy for them to send you referrals.
- Give them a referral, share a resource with them or be of value to them and you shall receive.
- Make quarterly connection calls or meetings.
- Provide them with your marketing collateral as a reminder of what you do.
- Engage with them on social sites.
- Give them a sample of what you offer or invite them to a demonstration of what you do.

Get permission to keep them up to date about your business via email or permission to engage on social media. Your goal is to deepen your relationship with them. The way I deepened my relationship with my NFL contacts was by inviting a key influencer to speak at my luncheon and be a guest on my radio show. Because I offered something important and valuable to her, she in turn recommended me to the Manager of the Emerging Business Program for the NFL.

A couple of months after that introduction, the manager called and hired me to deliver the keynote address at their final Emerging Business workshop, as well as to facilitate a networking session for over 200 attendees. That experience is a highlight in my professional career, and it would not have happened without a strategic plan and knowing how to leverage my local contacts.

Case Study

The owner of an event planning company attended a networking event I produced called M.I.N.G.L.E. Lunch & Learn. Her purpose for attending was to meet the guest speaker and get exposure for her business. She sat next to the speaker and gave her a business card. She also met two staffing agencies that wanted to form strategic alliances. A few weeks after the networking event, the speaker featured her business in the NFL Emerging Business newsletter. Now that's what I call networking at its best!

Step 7: Follow up and Follow Through

One of my biggest pet peeves is when people fail to follow through on their promise. It never ceases to amaze me how few business owners take the time to follow-up after they have made initial contact with a prospect. I can remember several occasions when I communicated that I needed services from someone I met, but they did not follow up. Once you've asked qualifying questions and identified that your lead is a good prospect, you'll want to implement your lead nurturing systems to get an appointment or close the sale. Lead nurturing helps you develop relationships with prospects at every stage of the sales cycle.

There is a variety of lead nurturing software on the market designed to help you launch top of mind awareness, welcome emails, product education, or promotional drip campaigns. Lead nurturing tools are all email-based campaigns. Don't miss out on new business because you are not effectively following up with your contacts.

Sort through that card holder and take the time to develop a system that works for you so that you can achieve the marketing goals you want. Enter them onto your lead management tool or customer relationship management (CRM) tool to keep track of the relationship and interactions. Follow up within 1 – 2 business days or on a date indicated during the initial meeting. An old-fashioned handwritten note or e-mail mentioning any personal details you learned is a nice touch. They will be impressed you remembered something about them.

The benefit of using a CRM tool is that it has features to help you nurture leads by keeping them engaged with your business through your email newsletter and social media. It also helps you with your follow up efforts.

Remember, not all contacts are worth pursuing. Create a lead scoring process to categorize which ones to focus on. Call top priority contacts to schedule a meeting to get to know more about their needs. Even if you get a no, it could simply mean that it's not a good time. Ask for a referral or ask them to sign up for your newsletter.

"I was in a situation in which I was meeting a lot of networkers but getting little results. I got help from Tarsha by reading her book "Beyond the Business Card." As a result, I have become more strategic and have gained more business. Now, I'm more effective, efficient, and profitable when conducting business for my company, A Turnaround Group. Tarsha, you are such a great help and I look forward to working with you more often."

Kevin Houston
Owner, A Turnaround Group

Chapter Summary

As the saying goes, a person who fails to plan, plans to fail. To make networking work for you, have a plan. Before you attend your next networking event, take 30 minutes to create your strategy. You will be intentional when networking; you'll save yourself a lot of time and you will leave feeling more confident you'll get business from the event.

Look at how you do networking on LinkedIn and Facebook to determine how you can incorporate the tips mentioned in this chapter. Remember to focus your social networking within groups to maximize your exposure and build relationships.

Lastly, be aware of how you network based on your personality. You might find the reason networking isn't effective for you is because of certain personality weaknesses or not understanding other personalities.

Go to http://bit.ly/PBactionplan2 and download a personal brand action plan to help you dive deeper into building your powerful brand.

(How can you use the lessons in this chapter create your networking plan? Use this page to write down your ideas and insights.)

CHAPTER TEN

The Brand Building Skills You Need

"We're all given some sort of skill in life. Mine just happens to be beating up on people."
Sugar Ray Leonard

BUILDING A POWERFUL brand requires skill. You must master a set of hard and soft skills to build a strong personal brand. Corporations have brand managers whose job is to be the "guardian" of the corporate brand. They maintain the brand's integrity across all marketing initiatives and communication channels. Just like a corporate brand manager, you are the guardian of your brand and responsible for creating a brand strategy to reach your target audience.

Recently, I received an email from a woman in the healthcare field. She mentioned listening to another coach talk about ways to build her practice. The coach told her she needed to learn to create a website, write a blog and create e-books. The start-up healthcare practitioner immediately did a Google search for "marketing coach for entrepreneurs" and guess who lands on the first page? Me, The Marketing Lady. She explained in her email how she had no idea how to do those things and wanted to know if I could teach her. Based on our conversation, I surmised that this woman didn't go to school to develop marketing skills; she went to school to study healthcare. Essentially, this woman is acting as the brand manager for her own personal brand but doesn't have the necessary skills to build it.

Most entrepreneurs getting started don't have the capital to pay experts to manage every aspect of building their brand, so they take the DIY (do-it-yourself) route to brand building. It takes effort and time to acquire the basic understanding of the skills someone else may have spent four to eight years in college developing. However, one can learn everything from graphic design to marketing campaign implementation.

Soft Skills and Hard Skills

Soft skills are tangible and not specific to one area of competency. Soft skills are interpersonal skills like communication, attitude, confidence and how to get along with others. Hard skills are teachable abilities like sales, marketing and accounting. Here's a list of the soft skills you need:

- Good verbal, non-verbal, and written communication skills. Whether you are a business owner or professional, you must be able to effectively communicate your brand's value, brand story, and competitive advantage.

- Public speaking is helpful in making presentations, connecting with your audience and establishing credibility.
- Rapport building is a necessity in brand building. Building rapport takes confidence, active listening skills and the ability to establish trust.
- Understanding your target audience, knowing their pain points and having a clear understanding of how your products/services solve their problems, is the business acumen skill you need to succeed.

In addition to mastering those soft skills you must also possess hard skills like planning, marketing, and selling.

- Brand managers are responsible for the overall brand strategy. Learning how to define goals and objectives then creating steps to implement those goals is a great hard skill to learn.
- Selling skills are helpful to solopreneurs who not only have to market the brand but must also be able to convert the leads that come from marketing.
- In the digital world we live in, you can't escape technology and design. Not even corporate brand managers know how to use all the technology or design software available, but they do understand what technology is needed to manage and communicate the brand. Some technology skills especially helpful in managing a brand include web and graphic design, social media, video creation, search engine optimization and mobile apps.
- I highly recommend that anyone taking the DIY marketing route learn a little bit about every aspect of marketing. Even though you won't be doing them all

yourself, you'll want to know what the marketing disciplines are, so you can make marketing decisions that increase your brand visibility.

Hire freelancers to help you with some of the hard skills and invest in courses to help you develop or improve your soft skills. What you decide to do yourself and what you choose to outsource is completely up to you. Evaluate your personal sales and marketing skills and get help where needed.

Use the Marketing and Skills Assessment below as follows. Check 'Yes' for items you feel capable of and comfortable doing. Check 'No' for items you feel you are _not_ capable of or are uncomfortable doing. Check 'Out' for items you want to outsource. If you are capable, but still would like to outsource, check 'Yes' and 'Out.'

Marketing and Skills Assessment	Yes	No	Out
Writing: Articles, case studies, social media, press releases, blogs, presentations, website content.			
Design/Layout: Designing a flyer/postcard, layout an e-book, creating infographics, creating graphical quotes for social media.			
Audio/Visual: Recording and/or editing audio in MP3 or MP4 format, taking high resolution photos, recording video via cell phone or video camera.			
Technology: Website updates, creating landing pages, creating webinars.			
Social Media Skills: Posting, reviewing analytics, scheduling/tracking posts and using social media management tools.			
Software Programs: Creating slides in PowerPoint documents in Publisher or Adobe, CRM programs and email marketing. Webinar tools.			
Speaking/Presenting: Speaking online/offline, presenting a topic, being interviewed via podcast or online radio.			
Project Management: Tracking and implementing tasks, managing outside vendors, creating a project timeline.			
Event Planning/Management: Organizing event online and offline, promoting the event and pulling together a team for the event.			
Selling/Networking: Creating a script, cold calling, networking to generate leads.			

While corporations have the human resources and financial resources for marketing a brand, most entrepreneurs do not. Having the right team of people and financial resources can make or break your brand building strategy. The list above may seem overwhelming. Narrow it down and focus on the top three brand building skills needed to enhance your brand identity and awareness. The three that have benefited me and many of my clients the most are the writing, communication and technology skills. When these three skills are mastered, they can help you create a strong brand in the marketplace.

Case Study

Susan is a licensed health and wellness coach with Your Invigorated Life. Like most entrepreneurs, she wanted to better understand how to market on social media. She didn't want to put in the time to figure out how to use social media for business and felt bogged down by the very thought of it. She lacked the skills needed to create content that would engage her audience and provide relevant content. After six coaching sessions with me, she learned how to write one 500-word article and create six pieces of content to post on social media. She realized that she could repurpose content, change it slightly and use it on different social media sites. By the end of the coaching program, Susan no longer felt social media was a scary monster. She felt confident and more in control of what to do for her social media strategy.

"Don't be afraid, Tarsha will walk you through it and make sense of everything!"

Susan J.
Your Invigorated Life

Chapter Summary

After reading this chapter you are probably thinking, "How in the world am I going to have a successful brand without the skills needed to build one?" My purpose was not to alarm you but make you aware of what is required to take your brand to a higher level. No one can build a successful brand alone. You need people who are talented in the areas you are not, so you can focus on delivering the brand's promise to your customers. However, to maintain the brand's integrity and communicate your brand effectively, you want to gain the soft and hard skills discussed in this chapter.

Do a self-evaluation and determine the brand building skills you will learn and what you will pay someone to do. Consider the amount of time and investment needed for you to learn the skills yourself. Remember, you are the guardian of your brand, so make wise marketing decisions like a brand manager.

Go to http://bit.ly/PBactionplan2 and download a personal brand action plan to help you dive deeper into building your powerful brand.

(How can you use the lessons in this chapter to improve your skills? Use this page to write down your ideas and insights.)

CHAPTER ELEVEN

Get Clear on Your Brand Message

"If you can't explain it to a 6-year old, you don't know it yourself."
Albert Einstein

O N MANY OCCASIONS I have worked with clients to redo their marketing. What I mean is, they put up a nice website, they have designed glossy marketing collateral and business cards or even pay for direct mail pieces to be sent. By the time they contact me, they've spent thousands of dollars and are still not getting leads or converting leads to sales. Brands struggle to create clear marketing messages and then say that marketing doesn't work. Oftentimes, the marketing activity is not to blame; instead, they failed to write messages in a way their customers can understand how their products and services will meet their needs, wants or desires. Their messages focus on selling the company's features instead of marketing the problem customers face and what things could be like if they use their brand.

Once, a realtor in my local area reached out to me for marketing advice. I won't say the company's name, but it is a real estate firm that has been in business for more than 15 years. When I first visited the website, I was confused because the name nor tagline of the company suggested that it was a residential real estate firm. My first thought was that it was a wealth management firm because the tagline reads, "Birthing Dreams, Building Legacies." If it weren't for the pictures of houses and the MLS search feature on the home page, I would not have thought "real estate." I'm not suggesting that the company name and tagline should have real estate in them, what I am saying is that customers can become confused if the words they read don't clearly communicate who you are, what you do, what problem you solve and the WIIFM (what's in it for me).

Examples like that are a frequent problem with solopreneurs who spend lots of money on marketing and branding, but none on messaging. Over the years I've encountered many brands struggling with the same issue. I started to realize that before I could help someone really create a powerful brand, I needed to help them get clear on their marketing messages. After conducting a lot research and getting advice from my mastermind group, SiSTARS, I decided to make some changes that I felt would give me the skills I needed to better meet the needs of my clients. I became certified in a storytelling technique. The technique is used by brands to tell their stories, making the customer the hero of their own story instead of the brand. It helps a company clarify its marketing messages.

In this chapter, I'm going to discuss how you can address the customer's problem, create clear marketing messages that address a customer's problem and why telling your brand story is an important marketing message. It will change the way you talk about your products and may even change the way you market your business. Your message matters and how you craft that message may determine whether a customer will take action.

In marketing, there are several models that marketers use to craft irresistible messages. The two I will cover are the P.S.B.A. and AIDA models.

Know Your Audience's Problems

The acronym P.S.B.A. stands for Problem, Solution, Benefit and Action. This model is widely used in business presentations, speeches, and developing marketing messages.

To effectively get your message across in the simplest way, define the customer's problem and how your brand solves it. In a previous chapter, I talked about creating a buyer persona. When you identify the pain points of your persona, you can market the customer's problem in your messages. You are going to need a clearer picture of who you are trying to attract with your messages to be able to answer these questions about your audience.

- What challenges, pain and uncertainty do they face?
- What can your company do to help your potential customers overcome a challenge and get what they really want?
- What is the main benefit of your solution to the customer?
- What would you like your customer to do once they understand how you solve their problem and what they will gain? What actions should they take?

In this example, I'm going to use the real estate firm I mentioned before. The message the agent was trying to get across was that buying a home is an investment and a way to build wealth for generations to come.

Problem Statement: Describe the problem, predicament or pain your target market is experiencing in terms that are meaningful to the person you are speaking with. *Example: Most people are paying the same amount in rent as a mortgage payment; yet it doesn't build them wealth, save them money on income taxes nor does it leave a legacy.*

Solution Statement: Tell them how you solve their problem. *Example: We help middle-income individuals buy a home they can afford and educate them on the benefits of homeownership compared to renting.*

Benefit Statement: Features tell but benefits sell. Tell them the benefits your clients will have by working with you or what success would look like. *Example: You will join the millions of homeowners that take advantage of the tax savings and wealth-building opportunities by buying instead of renting. Now you can have the lifestyle you've dreamed of.*

Action Statements: Tell or ask your customer to act. *Example: Attend one of our new homebuyer seminars and learn the advantages of being a homeowner.*

Crafting Your Signature Marketing Message

Now image if the real estate firm whose name and tagline is confusing had pictures on its website of individuals packing up their apartment and then getting the keys to a home. And, the opening paragraph on the website would say, *"At ABC Company we know that for the amount you pay in rent, you could own a home. A home is an investment in your future for generations to come. Our experienced agents have been in the local market for 20 years, so we can help you buy a home you can afford and educate you on the benefits of homeownership compared to renting. There are 300,000 homeowners in the Dallas area, and you can become the next one. Attend one of our free homebuyer seminars or contact us at 555-111-1234."*

Using this simple structure will help you get clear on your brand messages.

Awareness, Interest, Desire, Action

AIDA is a classic marketing communications model that identifies the stages an individual goes through during the buying process for a product or service. The acronym stands for Awareness, Interest, Desire and Action. Using this model will help you understand how your marketing communication message engages customers with your brand.

- Awareness: Your message must create awareness of your brand.
- Interest: Your message must entice someone's interest in the benefits of what you offer.
- Desire: Your message should appeal to their emotions.

- Action: Your message must get them to do something that would move them towards interacting with your brand.

Putting the AIDA Model to Work

To create *awareness*, use social media, your website, press announcements, advertising and events to get people aware of your brand and how you solve a problem. For example, a social media post with a picture of an apartment renter packing up a U-Haul beside a picture of that renter in front of their new home. The caption would say, "For what you pay in rent, you can own a home."

To create *interest*, create an enticing headline or title to grab attention. For example, a blog post on your website with the title, "Paying Too Much in Rent?"

Create *desire* through an emotional connection. For example, a post card mailer to apartment renters that reads, "Now you can have the lifestyle you've dreamed of by investing in home-ownership."

Get them to take *action*, by creating a sense of urgency or importance or getting them to do something. For example, you can place on the event landing page, "Register for a free home-buyer seminar. Only 20 spots available," or "Learn the advantages of homeownership on the event landing page."

You have two models to use in creating clear marketing messages. Pick the one you feel most comfortable using. Place your messages on all your marketing collateral, on your website, in your social media posts, in your speeches and video, and everywhere customers are exposed to your brand.

One Irresistible Message, Six Pieces of Content

Brainstorm with your team a list of problems your potential customers have, as it relates to what you offer. For each of those problems you will create an irresistible question followed by an irresistible title for your content. In this section, you'll need to review the problem, solution and benefit statements you created previously.

Here are some of the common problems my clients face:

Problem: I don't know how to attract opportunities that would position my company and brand at the top of mind with my target audience.

Irresistible Question: Are you ready to confidently communicate your brand value so that customers seek you out when they need your services?

Irresistible Title: Brand Confidence: How to Get Noticed so Clients Seek You Out

Now let's turn those irresistible messages into six pieces of marketing content that will help you stand out and get noticed.

1. Marketing Content Idea: [Blog] 7 Ways to Stay Top of Mind with Your Audience. Write a 300-500-word article using the title and post it on your website. Share the article to your social media pages and in your newsletter.
2. Marketing Content Idea: [Lead Generation Webinar] Brand Confidence: How to Get Noticed So Clients Seek

You Out. Host a free webinar using the title to build your email list.

3. Marketing Content Idea: [Email/Autoresponder Series] Why you should work with a coach to help you leverage social media and your local network to stand out and get noticed. Create an autoresponder series using the title and offer a free download of your e-book on the topic.

4. Marketing Content Idea: [Facebook Live] 3 Tips to Stand Out and Get Noticed. Do a Facebook Live broadcast and give tips from the article you wrote on the title.

5. Marketing Content Idea: [Social Media Graphics] Are You Ready to Communicate Your Brand Value with Confidence? Create a graphic that relates to the title and add one line of text to it. Post the graphic on your social media page with a call to action.

6. Marketing Content Idea: [Podcast] Host a podcast and interview someone on the title that you wrote.

Telling Your Brand Story

Whether you want to write a speech or create a video about your company, stories will help you connect and engage with your audience. Telling your brand story is more than what you tell people, it encompasses many of the things we've covered in this book: your mission and vision, what you do and who you do it for, and why you do what you do. Story is the single most important factor in selling your brand's value proposition. Stories draw people in. Think about the last movie you saw or motivational speech you heard; didn't the story draw you in? Stories motivate and inspire people to think, feel, be, or do something.

People relate to stories. When listening to stories people can sometimes see themselves in the situation and can validate certain feelings they have. How many times have you been hanging out with friends or family and a story about someone or something started? People like to share stories even with strangers. Most importantly for a brand, stories get people to take action. Donald Miller, CEO of Story Brand and author, calls story a sense-making device. When you have a complicated message you want to convey, tell it in a story and they will understand. One of my previous clients, Timmy Newsome is a former Dallas Cowboy. He now owns a technology firm. When he meets with companies to do sales pitches, he explains computer networking using sports as an analogy. He tells stories about his days as a Cowboy and the plays they use to run. These plays are used as examples of how computer network systems work. The stories he tells help him connect with the potential buyer, build trust, respect and a common interest.

Why Story is Important in Marketing

Customers want to interact with brands they like and form a relationship. However, 83% of consumers are unsatisfied with their relationship with brands.[11] Cultivating a relationship includes sharing your brand story in an authentic and genuine way. Building a relationship with the customer means your brand must show some vulnerability. Domino's Pizza's apology campaign is a great example of this. They were receiving criticism from customers regarding the taste of its pizza. Instead of ignoring the feedback they decided to acknowledge it and apologize to its customers.[12] The campaign featured the CEO of Domino's apologizing, it showed behind the scenes of employees reading the poor comments, and they even went to the homes of their customers to get them to try the new pizza. [13]In that campaign, Domino's told its brand story—who they were, why they were there to help the customer, and why they should be given another try. It demonstrated their vulnerability and confidence as a brand.

Understanding the structure of storytelling is important to writing a clear message that connects with your audience. Storytelling Navigator, Star Bobatoon, uses a simple structure called, Once Upon a Time: "Once upon a time, and then, but now." Author of *Building a Story Brand*, Donald Miller uses this structure: "A character with a problem meets a guide. The guide gives them a plan and tells them to take action. Their actions result in a success or failure."

Try this exercise with your brand. Write a brief statement for each of the following and then frame it as a story.

- Is there anything interesting about how your company was started, or about its founder(s)?
- What is the problem you are solving for your customer?
- What makes your brand the authority to solve this problem and how will your brand help them through their challenges?
- How can the customer be seen as the hero of the story?
- What are the consequences of not using your solution to solve their problem?
- How can you tell in a story what success would look like for the customer?

You shouldn't have to waste money on marketing that doesn't work for you. Implement the examples provided to get clear on your brand messages. Now, your website won't be confusing, your marketing collateral will be clear, and your speeches will engage and connect with your audience. Then, you will have a better return on your marketing dollars.

Chapter Summary

It is important that you learn to connect with your audience so you can share your messages in an authentic, relevant and meaningful way. When you do this, your marketing efforts becomes powerfully irresistible. When your message addresses the customer's problem, it will draw and attract your ideal clients, thus giving you a willing, ready, and able audience eager to pay for your products and services. Both the P.S.B.A. and AIDA models will help you get clear on your brand messages. Use storytelling techniques to share something that people care about and want to buy into. It's about framing your brand and dictating your value using story.

Go to http://bit.ly/PBactionplan2 and download a personal brand action plan to help you dive deeper into building your powerful brand.

(How can you use the lessons in this chapter to write clear marketing messages? Use this page to write down your ideas and insights.)

CHAPTER TWELVE

When to Reinvent Your Brand

"I feel like I have a job to do, like I constantly have to reinvent myself. The more I up the ante for myself, the better it is in the long run."

Kevin Hart

2018 WAS A year of many personal and business challenges. At the beginning of the year one-fourth of my company's revenues were loss. One of my clients no longer had the funding to hire me as an independent contractor. Although I knew it was coming, I didn't prepare and failed to replace that contract with another one before it ended. In the 15 years of being an entrepreneur, I had never experienced that big of a loss before. But that wasn't the only setback I experienced that year. A tragic death followed by health-related deaths happened in my family, and I also experienced health issues that impacted my ability to perform certain tasks. With slow to no paying clients, clients going out of business and personal challenges, I felt a lot of stress and anxiety. When you are a personal brand, you must constantly show up the way you want to be known. When the unexpected happens, it's hard to do that. I found myself contemplating my next move.

I thought to myself, how can I reinvent The Marketing Lady just like I did when I started Pivotal Marketing Group? What could I do to propel my brand to new heights? How can I leverage the brand and reputation the Marketing Lady built over the past 15 years? I needed to reinvent myself, again.

Brand Reinvention

When brands reinvent themselves, they change what they do or the way they do things so their audience can think of them differently. Brands reinvent when sales are slow or dropping, they may reinvent when how they do things is outdated or even when customer satisfaction is low. They start to look at things, like the product line, to see how they can change or improve it. Brands evaluate its target customer to determine if they should continue to serve that market or move on to another and they evaluate its packaging to determine if it needs a facelift.

Back in the day (in the 80s), I remember watching my grandfather shave, then he'd use his *Old Spice* aftershave lotion. I can't remember the commercials from back then, but in 2010 Old Spice launched an advertising campaign called "The Man Your Man Could Smell Like." The campaign was a way to reinvent the brand by promoting its new product lines to a different audience than it had in the 1960s. [14]

One of the biggest brand reinventions you may recall is the Yellow Pages and White Pages. I can remember those two big books being delivered to my doorstep. When I needed to search for a local business or residential phone number, I would flip through the pages. The Internet is what forced what was one of the most popular and affordable forms of advertising for a local business to reinvent itself. Advances in online technology and mobile devices meant people no longer needed to use the books. They would use their computers or mobile phones instead. Luckily, Yellow Pages was able to reinvent the way in which they provided their products to its end users. [15]

Reinvent Your Brand by First Looking Internally

- Evaluate your current customers. What are customers saying that could be a clue on how you need to reinvent? Failing to listen to customers can be detrimental to sales. Your current customer data can tell you helpful things about them, such as their purchase behaviors and preferences. Use the data you collect on customers to improve your service and their experience, determine new products/services to offer or items to upsell. For example, my past client, Exotic Hair Collection realized many of her customers were hair stylists who were purchasing her hair extensions for their own clients. Now she offers a special purchasing program for people to buy wholesale.

- Evaluate your sales. If they are stagnating or declining, it's probably a good time to get your team together or hire a firm to brainstorm ways to improve your product or services to increase sales. Are there certain product or service lines that is not producing well? It may be time to drop that line and focus your marketing efforts on the ones that bring in higher sales.

- Evaluate your image. Sometimes a stale brand needs to revamp its image. Your personal brand image is what people see, how you carry yourself, the way you dress, and your online presence. Your image is also the depiction of your strengths, values, and passions. I try to wear my brand colors as much as possible when I have speaking engagements. The way I dress is a representation of my personality and is consistent with how my brand is represented online, in print, or in person. How are you showing up in the world? Is what people experience online and offline with you the same? Your reinvention could start with projecting a different image.

Reinvent Your Brand by Looking Externally

- Re-evaluate your target market, just like the makers of *Old Spice* who wanted to capture a new audience of buyers. They listened to what men wanted and improved their product line and packaging. Conduct a focus group or survey to determine what your audience's wants and needs are and how those wants and needs relate to your offer. Jane Atkinson, a well-known speaker coach spent six years working for a speaker's bureau as an agent and manager. She reinvented herself by changing the target audience. Instead of helping meeting planners locate speakers for events, she now helps speakers launch successful speaking businesses.
- Review changes in the environment, your industry and technology and how they affect your brand. One of my

former clients has been in the leadership training industry for 38 years. As you can image, much has changed in the industry and with technology over time. To remain relevant and attract the attention of younger generations, this client had to make some shifts in how training was delivered. They had to incorporate more social media and conduct webinars to be in line with what others were doing in the leadership training industry.

For a personal brand, reinvention happens when there is a major shift in your life—like losing a loved one, divorce, unhappiness with current circumstances, or significant business losses. You are ready for a transformation. You are ready to leave the shape you are in to get to the S.H.A.P.E you want your brand to become in order to reach full potential.

So how do you do this, you ask? You must move from your *now* brand shape into your *new* brand S.H.A.P.E, an acronym for Specialness, Heart, Attitude, Potential, and Expertise.

- **S is Specialness** – Perhaps you developed a unique process or solution that disrupts things in your industry or a system for improving your work. When you reinvent yourself around your "specialness" it gives you the edge and you're in charge of creating your possibilities. Assess your personal brand to determine what makes you special. Ask 10 of your closest friends and/or colleagues to pick out the attributes that best describe you and reinvent yourself in one of those areas. For example, if people see you as being confident, then coach others on how to be more confident. You've reinvented yourself as a confidence coach.

- **H is Heart** –Your heart's passion is what motivates you, gets you going! You may already know that without passion you'll have trouble overcoming obstacles along your journey. Your passion will:
  - Attract employers, business partners and clients to you
  - Inspire others to see your vision
  - Increase your confidence
  - Help you to be persistent in your purpose

Heart is the area in which I've most recently reinvented myself. I've always been passionate about entrepreneurship. My first entrepreneurial experience started in middle school while in Junior Achievement. Junior Achievement is a nonprofit youth organization that fosters work-readiness, financial literacy and entrepreneurial skills in children grades K-12. Our team had to create a product and develop a plan to sell that product. I was the VP of Public Relations. My job was to help get the word out about our product in the community. That was my first marketing related role.

Since middle school, I've held leadership roles in business and/or entrepreneurial organizations. I helped start the Collin County Black Chamber of Commerce in McKinney, Texas. I was the chapter president of the Dallas/Ft. Worth National Association of Women Business Owners. I've traveled the country and abroad speaking on marketing and business topics to entrepreneurs. I've coached and trained hundreds of entrepreneurs starting a business. I volunteer with Junior Achievement to give back to an organization that planted the entrepreneurial seed in me.

My passion for entrepreneurship has led me to a new way to reinvent myself. Today, I serve as the director of the LiftFund Dallas/Ft. Worth Women's Business Center where I'm able to empower women to become successful entrepreneurs. You hear about this type of reinvention all the time. Someone leaves a career or role to pursue their passion. Make a list of the things you are passionate about and ask yourself, how can I reinvent myself to do what I love to do?

- **A is Attitude** – As you reinvent yourself you must have an attitude of success. What I mean is that you must carry the attitude of what your brand is meant to be, not what it *use* to be.

Years ago, while working part-time at a non-profit microlending organization where I provided business counseling, I had a client who had a hard time getting good employment because of his past circumstances. He decided to get a barber's license, so he could create his own employment opportunities. Instead of feeling defeated and blaming others, he had an attitude of success. He started a barber salon. Today, 10dollarhaircuts.com is a community-focused barbershop that offers affordable haircuts to a community that may not be able to afford a quality haircut. You see, when you have the right attitude, you are destined to achieve your goals. Make a list of the attitudes you'd have to change in order to have a success mindset. Work with a life coach to help you make a mindset shift so you can leave your old shape behind.

- **P is Potential** – Nothing will get you to where you want to be better than understanding how to plug into your potential. Your potential is rooted in what you are naturally great at. Your potential is about your identity—who do you see yourself as? It's about your importance—what impact can you make in someone's life or in the world? It's your purpose. It's your *why*.

Without purpose you have no direction for your brand. Without purpose, how can you define success? Without purpose how can you express your brand to the world? When you know the answers to those questions about yourself, you see the glass half-full instead of half-empty. To reinvent yourself and get what it is that you want, you are going to have to **B.E.C.O.M.E.** a powerful brand. And here's how:

Become the person you want to be.

Evaluate the characteristics and habits of successful people and learn from them.

Conduct your life centered around your values.

Own it. Have confidence in yourself and your ability to do your job.

Market your brand in your field and in the community.

Expect success. Success will come when you incorporate successful activities that move you towards your goals.

"The will to win, the desire to succeed, the urge to reach your full potential...these are the keys that will unlock the door to personal excellence."

Confucius

- **E is Expertise** – To be a successful brand, it is best to find opportunities that put your best skills to use. Regardless of what product or service you are offering, you must demonstrate your expertise in that given field. Here's an example of how to reinvent yourself based on your expertise. One of my clients, who works in the healthcare industry, had a near death experience. She used her experience to develop resources to educate people about end of life planning. What started out as a passion project based on life experience propelled her into a new role as a sought-after thought leader in the field of end of life planning. For small business owners and those looking to develop their personal brands, increasing your brand authority as an expert is a necessary step towards brand reinvention. Make a list of all the things you do well, list the industries you are the authority in and why. Then evaluate your list to determine how you can reinvent yourself based on skills or expertise you haven't tapped into yet.

Becoming a thought leader in your niche or industry is all about establishing yourself as someone worth paying attention to. It is a method of marketing yourself as an expert or authority in your industry. You must learn to think of yourself as a brand in your own right, not just as a company brand. You should strive to have instant name recognition by industry leaders in your niche. If we say the names Steve Jobs, Bill Gates, or Mark Zuckerberg, most people will know who we are talking about and what industry they serve.

Becoming a thought leader in your niche industry may take some time and effort, but the financial and professional rewards can be well worth it in the long run.

Reinvent Yourself as a Thought Leader in Your Industry

- Do your industry research. Where do people interested in your expertise spend their time and money? What social networks do they visit? What do they talk about? What are their pain points and problems in relation to the area you are the authority in? What solutions are they willing to pay for and how much will they pay? Who are your main competitors and how good are their products? What are customers saying about those products? Can you come up with even better ones?

- Create great content. The goal of thought leadership marketing is not to write *salesy* content, but to write content that addresses the readers problems and positions you as the expert. Use your research to create content readers and followers want. People learn visually most of the time but offering a range of content gives them a choice. The more content you create, especially free content, the more traffic you will get from search engines and social sites. Seeing your name and (good) content appearing repeatedly will make potential customers check you and your offering out more closely.

- Connect on social media. The secret to success in social media is in the name itself: social. People are on social networks to connect with others, not to see your latest promotion. However, people are always on the lookout for products and services that make their lives easier. Be helpful in all your interactions and people will appreciate and remember what you do for them. Make the most of groups. Are there social media groups you can join to connect with your target audience and other like-minded people? Facebook and LinkedIn have some very active groups.

- Convert connections. Rather than focusing on quantity of posts, tweets, and pins to convert your connections into email subscribers, focus on quality. Use the information you gained from your research and insights to provide a special offer that is specific to your followers on a particular social media platform. For example, a healthy eating consultant could provide an exclusive and free offer, available only to Instagram followers who sign up for recipe ideas during a specific time. Now, she has converted her Instagram followers into email subscribers where she can nurture the leads.

- Using thought leadership marketing to establish your personal brand can take time. However, the sooner you get started, the faster you will begin to reap the rewards.

Developing a personal leadership brand can increase your level of credibility and propel you to new heights. The "P" in S.H.A.P.E. stands for Potential. One area that a personal brand may have great potential is in how they lead. Have you given any thought to building your leadership brand as a way to reinvent yourself?

What is Leadership Branding?

Many entrepreneurs and career professionals want to build a personal brand, but few pay any attention to their leadership brand. Not to be confused with brand leadership, a personal leadership brand according to Harvard Business Review is your distinct characteristics as a leader that have an impact on the work you do. Your value becomes known for that distinction among your network, clients and colleagues. [16]

I have held many leadership board roles over the years. I was chapter president of Dallas Urban League Young Professionals and of the National Association of Women Business Owners in Dallas. I have served on the board of directors for four nonprofits, on the Mayor's Small Business Task Force, and on an advisory committee. In these roles, I was in alignment with my personal mission and vision; they were aligned with my goals; and I was passionate about the causes. Being in leadership roles helped to raise my profile, established my leadership style and helped me establish relationships with influencers in the small business community. While serving in these roles, I was cultivating a leadership brand to maintain the positive aspects of me that would create a positive brand perception of me. The truth of the matter is that one person's perception of you becomes their reality. Don't let people have the wrong perception of your brand.

Your leadership brand is your approach to how you run your business, interact with employees or colleagues and behave in challenging situations. So, what might be the distinct characteristics that shape your leadership brand? Let's look at some fundamental leadership characteristics.

- Leaders have vision. They have a clear sense of what direction they want their brand to go.
- Leaders have passion. The leader that is passionate or excited about their vision will get others enthusiastic as well.
- Leaders motivate and inspire. Leadership is not about telling people what to do; it's about inspiring people to get things done.

- Leaders have values they live by and are known for.

To better define your leadership brand, think about the attributes you rely on to achieve results. Strategic, collaborative, inspiring, and creative thinker are a few attributes that come to mind for me. I recommend getting a 360° personal brand assessment done so you can see the effectiveness and perception others have of your leadership brand. This eye-opening experience may help you recognize areas where you can reinvent your brand.

Make a list of your core strengths you want to be known for as a leadership brand and then write down your catchphrase. For me, *I want to be known for inspiring others to make an impact through their personal brand and developing strategies for them to live their entrepreneurial dreams.* This statement is different from your elevator pitch, in that it puts an emphasis on who you are more than what you offer. When coming up with your catchphrase, include your attributes, make it sound authentic and make it interesting enough that the reader would want to learn more about you.

The statement you create is the statement you can reinvent your brand identity around. Let's say a female senior level manager in the IT industry has an attribute of confidence. She notices that other women in IT seem intimidated and lack confidence to take the lead on projects. Through this observation, she decides to quit her job and become a confidence coach to help women in the IT profession build more confidence so they can advance their careers. Now, she has reinvented herself and is known for something else. Now her catchphrase might sound like this, "I use my keen insight and collaborative approach to motivate female IT professionals to gain the confidence they need to increase their standing in the industry. I'm dedicated to helping them understand their worth." Now this confidence coach is establishing a reputation for what she will be known.

Share your leadership brand in the community, with your employees, with your colleagues and your online profiles. Take a close look at everything you do as a leader, and ask yourself, "Am I expressing what I want to be known for? Does my title represent what I want to be known for?"

Titles Mean Something

Job titles help to indicate the organizational structure and functions within the company. But how important are titles for personal brands? Expert, strategist, consultant, speaker, author, coach, owner, CEO, president—all speak to knowledge, expertise and level of success. So, choosing the right title when you reinvent your brand will define your position in the marketplace and establish your credibility.

As a personal brand, I've always looked at titles to define what I do or what I'm good at. During my entire entrepreneurial career, I've given myself titles like Marketing Consultant, Speaker, Author, Coach, and Personal Brand Strategist because they describe what I do or who I am. The title you create for your personal brand can increase your visibility on social media.

I did a LinkedIn advanced search to see how many personal brands in my local Dallas network used the titles I used.

> *Personal Brand = 2 results (me and 1 other person)*
> *Strategist = 50 results*
> *Author = 76 results*
> *Speaker = 129 results*
> *Coach = 143 results*
> *Consultant = 354 results*

Now that I have a new title, I advanced searched for Director on LinkedIn; there were 446 results (including me). During a 7-day time span, my profile appeared in search results 191 times using keywords marketing specialist, marketing director, project manager, and adjunct instructor.

Weekly search stats

191

number of times your profile appeared in search results between February 12 - February 19

Figure 2
Weekly Search Statistics

Your LinkedIn search appearance results can tell you many things. It tells you who's viewed your profile and the key terms used to find you.

Keywords your searchers used

Marketing Director

Coach

National Sales Director

Director

Author

⊚ Want to improve future search appearances?

Figure 3
Key Terms

This is helpful because it lets you know if your profile is reaching the right audience and if you have the right keywords and headline on your profile to reach them. The results tell you what the searcher does for a living, what industry they are in and the company they are with.

Use LinkedIn to help you build brand awareness by posting articles, using hashtags with your posts, recording videos and engaging on LinkedIn influencers' posts. Be sure your profile is optimized, meaning you have a professional profile photo, a keyword-focused headline, and a summary that includes what you want to be known for that tells your story. Your summary should also include keywords you want people to search to help find you. Give and get recommendations and endorsements. Recommendations from clients, vendors, or employees will help validate your reputation as a leadership brand and the endorsements help you become known for a skillset. Lastly, show off your expertise. LinkedIn allows you to upload your work to showcase. You can upload slides, videos, and pdf documents.

My Reinvention

In October 2018, I reinvented myself and transitioned to a career with a nonprofit organization as the director of its Women's Business Center. You're probably wondering how and why I made the transition. Let me explain. While I was president of the Dallas Chapter of National Association of Women's Business Owners (NAWBO), an employee who worked at the nonprofit approached me to request I write a letter of support for the organization to receive a grant to open the center. As the chapter president of a women's business organization, I could not refuse. At that time, I had no intention of working for the organization, I just wanted to lend my support of seeing a women's business center in Dallas.

Several months passed and I had not heard if they received the grant. Six months later, I was talking on the phone with a client who informed me that the organization had won the grant four months prior. They were looking for a director to open and manage the center. She felt I would make a great candidate because of my work building the NAWBO DFW chapter and my experience coaching entrepreneurs and helping brands market themselves. The irony of it all is this: I'd done business with this organization in the past, a previous client of mine also knows their CEO, and my letter played a part in them winning the grant. Can you say this role had my name on it? After the trials and tribulations, I experienced in 2018, personally and professionally, I trusted my instincts and followed my passion for entrepreneurship.

People will place you on a pedestal based on your title. I'll admit, I was a little shocked by what this new title would afford me. I have been invited to more events as a VIP guest, asked to speak on more panels than I was before and the requests for interviews have increased. Mind you, before the new title I had been doing these things for over a decade. The same thing I do as the director of the DFW Women's Business Center by LiftFund, I did for over 1,000 businesses in a 16-year span. I am leveraging many of the same contacts and resources I developed as an entrepreneur in my new role. My level of credibility and influence has increased and, most importantly, my personal brand has become more powerful and impactful.

While I still have my brand, The Marketing Lady, it is reinvented into more than a personal brand strategist. It is being positioned to make an impact in the lives of women and minorities in the DFW area. Brand reinvention can come in many ways, whether it's making a transition, changing directions or starting all over, you should consider your Specialness, Heart, Attitude,

Potential, and Expertise (S.H.A.P.E.) and share it with the world. Address your weaknesses and bad habits. To truly reinvent yourself, you must minimize the unhealthy attributes that could jeopardize you from reaching your destiny.

You must have a vision of the future you want to create because when you visualize, you materialize. Ask yourself, what do I really want? How do you want your life to be? Have goals and the steps you plan to take to reach them. Our goals help us chart the course. Have supporting goals for every piece of the vision. Stay positive and motivated by aligning your environment to support your new S.H.A.P.E. Hang around positive people, read positive affirmations. Why? Because obstacles will try to block the path to your dreams, and you need to be motivated to stay on track.

Chapter Summary

Now you know what reinventing yourself is all about. Reinventing your personal brand by creating a new S.H.A.P.E. is a good place to start. Look internally and externally to ensure you are reinventing in the best way. Create a personal image that reflects your S.H.A.P.E. Create a motto or tag line you go by. Branding yourself gives you a leg up on your peers. You must understand what your leadership brand is and develop a title and catchphrase to support it. And, don't underestimate what a title can mean to your personal brand when you reinvent yourself.

Lastly, be authentic. Be who you are and not what others think you are.

Go to http://bit.ly/PBactionplan2 and download a personal brand action plan to help you dive deeper into building your powerful brand.

(How can you use the lessons in this chapter to reinvent your brand?
Use this page to write down your ideas and insights.)

Notes

[1] https://www.shopify.com/tools/business-name-generator

[2] https://www.forbes.com/sites/petercarbonara/2018/06/06/worlds-largestretail-companies-2018/#404f25e113e6

[3] https://www.fastcompany.com/1690654/blockbuster-bankruptcy-decadedecline

[4] https://www.sba.gov/tools/sizeup

[5] https://www.blogtalkradio.com/letstalksuccess

[6] http://bit.ly/superbowl45NTX

[7] https://www.facebook.com/business/help/148723649153231

[8] https://www.facebook.com/business/news/ insights/shiftsfor-2020-multisensory-multipliers

[9] https://blog.bufferapp.com/influencer-marketing-cost

[10] https://www.meetup.com/Evolving-Women/events/10371415/

[11] https://www.adweek.com/digital/study-83-percent-of-consumers-unsatisfied-by-relationships-with-brands/

[12] https://youtu.be/AH5R56jILag

[13] https://youtu.be/A-lphVQkM1s

[14] https://en.wikipedia.org/wiki/The_Man_Your_Man_Could_Smell_Like

[15] https://www.cnbc.com/2015/12/22/four-iconicbrands-that-reinvented-themselves.html?slide=1

[16] https://hbr.org/2010/03/define-your-personalleadership

Personal Brand Resources

Personal Brand Online Workshop

This book is packed with ideas and techniques you can use to build a powerful personal brand. If you would like help, the personal brand online workshop will walk you through the steps outlined in the book so you can make an impact with your brand. The online course has a downloadable workbook to guide you through the process. Get the workshop at buildapowerfulpersonalbrand.com.

Personal Brand Action Plan

A five-page document that asks you powerful questions to get you thinking about what your personal brand really is. Download your copy here http://bit.ly/PBactionplan2.

Personal Brand Private Session

From the comfort of your office or in our Dallas office, we can customize a personal brand strategy that aligns with your goals and helps you grow your brand. You'll spend 1.5 days with our team, and you'll leave with a blueprint for your personal brand.

7 Steps to an Irresistible Brand Kit

Sign up at www.themarketinglady.com to receive a six-page step-by-step personal brand guide, a personal brand profile template, and a 30-minute "How to Stand Out from the Crowd" audio. Plus, a 15-day trial account to 360Reach™ Personal Branding Assessment tool.

ABOUT THE AUTHOR

Tarsha Polk, The Marketing Lady, is a personal brand strategist, international speaker and author of the book, *Beyond the Business Card: Strategic Networking for Success*. Her entrepreneurial endeavors started in 2003 when she formed a marketing firm to assist companies with innovative marketing solutions. She has helped more than 1,000 individuals with their marketing and business strategies. Tarsha has spent the last 20 years building a powerful personal brand. She has received numerous awards such as,

Business of the Year, 40 Under 40, Who's Who of Black Dallas, and the Women's Leadership award. Her business acumen and brand presence led to winning a contract with the NFL for Super Bowl XLV, where she was hired to facilitate a networking session and deliver the keynote address. A former Internet radio show host and marketing columnist, Tarsha provided marketing tips and business advice to business owners across the Dallas/Ft. Worth area and to thousands online. She's been featured in national publications like *Black Enterprise* as well as the local Dallas Business Journal.

When Googled, her brand The Marketing Lady, dominates the first page of the search results. Her name "Tarsha Polk" is prevalent on the first ten pages. An engaging and inspirational professional speaker, she has spoken in 42 states and abroad on marketing and business topics.

Because of her passion to empower people to succeed in business, she volunteers her expertise with organizations that train military veterans and high school students on entrepreneurship.